HOME OFFICE RESEARCH STUDY NO. 108

Drinking and Disorder:
A Study of
Non-Metropolitan Violence

by Mary Tuck

A HOME OFFICE
RESEARCH AND PLANNING UNIT
REPORT

LONDON: HER MAJESTY'S STATIONERY OFFICE

© *Crown copyright 1989*
First published 1989

ISBN 0 11 340926 5

HOME OFFICE RESEARCH STUDIES

"Home Office Research Studies" comprise reports on research undertaken in the Home Office to assist in the exercise of its administrative functions, and for the information of the judicature, the services for which the Home Secretary has responsibility (direct or indirect) and the general public.

On the last pages of this report are listed titles already published in this series, in the preceding series Studies in the Causes of Delinquency and the Treatment of Offenders, and in the series of Research and Planning Unit Papers.

Her Majesty's Stationery Office

Standing order service

Placing a standing order with HMSO BOOKS enables a customer to receive other titles in this series automatically as published.

This saves time, trouble and expense of placing individual orders and avoids the problem of knowing when to do so.

For details please write to HMSO BOOKS (PC13A/1), Publications Centre, PO Box 276, London, SW8 5DT and quoting reference X25.08.07.

The standing order service also enables customers to receive automatically as published all material of their choice which additionally saves extensive catalogue research. The scope and selectivity of the service has been extended by new techniques, and there are more than 3,500 classifications to choose from. A special leaflet describing the service in detail may be obtained on request.

Foreword
and Acknowledgements

Although my name is the only one on the title page of this report, my main responsibility has been in the design and writing up of the study. The research it records was a co-operative endeavour which involved many people in both the private and public sectors.

The design of the study was hammered out in discussion by staff of the Home Office Research and Planning Unit with special expertise in studies of disorder, policing, crime prevention and alcohol consumption patterns. Lizanne Dowds, Paul Ekblom, Tom Ellis, Tim Hope, Peter Southgate, Joy Mott and Roy Walmsley all made important contributions.

Tim Hope and Tom Ellis of the Research and Planning Unit took responsibility for commissioning the locational analysis recorded in Chapter 2 and for much background statistical work. The analyses themselves were carried out by CACI Market Analysis Ltd and we would like to thank Keith Dugmore of that firm for his many important contributions.

Peter Southgate of the Research and Planning Unit took responsibility for commissioning the observational work recorded in Chapter 3 of the report. This was carried out by a commercial company, Accent Marketing and Research. We would like to thank the seven fieldworkers involved, Gillian Davies, Chris O'Donovan, Tim Grosvenor, Dee Levy, Mike Rogers, Jackie Taylor and Neville Woodhead for some very detailed and careful field notes and also for their many insights. Tim Grosvenor of Accent made a particularly useful contribution.

Lizanne Dowds of the Research and Planning Unit took responsibility for commissioning the survey and group discussions reported on in Chapter 4. These were carried out by Research Surveys of Great Britain Ltd and we would like to thank particularly Philip Mercieca who managed the survey and Bob Lucas who carried out the group discussions. Justin Russell of the Research and Planning Unit assisted in calculations on the survey data.

Paul Ekblom of the Research and Planning Unit took responsibility for the police message pad analyses referred to in Chapters 3 to 5. He was assisted by Diane Caddle and Hugh Robertson of the Unit. Tom Ellis of the Research and Planning Unit was responsible for the collation and organisation of the statistical appendices to the study.

Over 20 people were involved in this research and many of them provided detailed written accounts of their work, frequently quoted directly. The Research and Planning Unit staff involved have also commented extensively on early drafts of this report.

So the present study is very genuinely a group effort. That a study of this complexity could be put in hand, completed and reported on within a few months is, I believe, a tribute to the effectiveness of the small team of experts within the Home Office Research and Planning Unit and to their skills in collaborating with the private sector. I would like to thank my colleagues.

MARY TUCK
Head of the Research and Planning Unit

Contents

1 The research problem and the research design

In the early nineteen eighties, the most salient public order problem in the United Kingdom was the problem of violence and riots in the cities. It was not until the summer of 1988 that the problem of "rural" or "non-metropolitan" violence became a focus of widespread public concern.

Concern about public disorder or drunkenness in non-metropolitan areas had, of course, existed before the summer of 1988. Home Office Ministers had drawn attention to the problem in public speeches in the later part of 1987 and the early part of 1988. The profile of the problem was, however, raised sharply in June of that year by the publication of a joint press release from three police associations – the Association of Chief Police Officers, the Superintendents' Association and the Police Federation – representing all police officers in England and Wales. This press release, "Police Speak Out on Violence and Disorder", described a survey – "Public Disorder Outside Metropolitan Areas" – which had been carried out by Mr Brian Hayes, Chief Constable of Surrey, on behalf of the Association of Chief Police Officers, with the co-operation of the Home Office. As the press release put it:—

'A special police survey, details of which are released this week, reveals an alarming picture of nationwide disorder in once-tranquil small towns and rural areas in England and Wales. The issue is currently being discussed by senior officers and Home Office officials.

No longer is spontaneous disorder confined to inner cities and large towns. Groups of usually young and often drunk people gather to fight each other, and to attack police and property in a way that was a rarity even as recently as ten years ago.'

The survey document on which the press release was based has not itself been publicly released. It was felt there could be disadvantages in listing in a public document those towns or villages where public order was already experienced as a problem by the police. It was, of course, available to the Home Office and immediately the press release on the survey was published the Home Secretary commented that "the ACPO survey, carried out in consultation with the Home Office, is a very useful examination of the extent of this serious problem" and drew attention to his own concern about this issue, as recorded in speeches made earlier that year.

The ACPO survey called for further research on the phenomenon it documented. It had established that during 1987 public disorder was a widespread problem in county forces, that the presence of young men was a key element among those involved and arrested and that alcohol featured powerfully in the disorder,

1

being mentioned in over 90% of the reported incidents. It raised the question "why is this type of behaviour happening with such frequency?" and commented, "the question is not one that police officers alone can realistically attempt to answer properly, but it may be an area which can be fruitfully explored by others, particularly bearing in mind the distribution of activity identified by the study". (ACPO 1988).

On receiving the ACPO study, the Home Secretary immediately called for further research addressed to the topic this identified. This research fell to the Home Office Research and Planning Unit to organise and carry out. It is this work which is reported in this document.

Method

The starting point was, of course, the ACPO report itself. This had listed all incidents reported by Chief Constables for the year 1987 where group violence had occurred, which needed reinforcement of ten or more officers in addition to normal sub-divisional patrol strength and where experience indicated that difficulty occurred in mobilising that level of reinforcement in sufficient time. Only incidents taking place *outside* metropolitan areas were collated.

Although many early comments on the ACPO findings assumed that it described "rural" violence, it is important to realise that it covered all incidents across England and Wales which were not within Police Force Metropolitan Areas. Map 1 opposite shows these metropolitan areas. It will immediately be seen that not all non-metropolitan areas could conceivably be called "rural"; "metropolitan areas" are quite narrowly defined. "Non-metropolitan areas" include such sizeable towns as Nottingham, Blackpool or Brighton together with a multitude of smaller towns, larger villages and densely settled areas, although they also include areas which could genuinely be called "rural".

Realising these complexities, the ACPO report called for "studies conducted outside the service on the sociological and demographic issues that are apparent in the regional pattern identified" in their study, and with this in mind ACPO made available to the Home Office the full results of their 1987 survey. It seemed a first priority to carry out a thorough locational analysis on the ACPO incident list to see if some particular type of area could be identified in which these incidents clustered. The findings of this locational analysis are covered in Chapter 2 of this report.

It was further decided to select from the locational analysis, three specific places which had experienced serious problems in 1987 and to match these with three other areas, which the computer analysis showed to be similar on socio-demographic variables, but which had not recorded problems in 1987 (the exact methodology by which these sites were selected is described at the beginning of Chapter 3). Fieldwork was arranged for two weeks in each of these six sites to cover observation of local drinking patterns and any resulting disorder and interviews with local figures such as police, licensees and magistrates. These

2

Map 1 Metropolitan and Non-Metropolitan Areas of England Wales

STANDARD REGIONS AND COUNTIES OF ENGLAND AND WALES

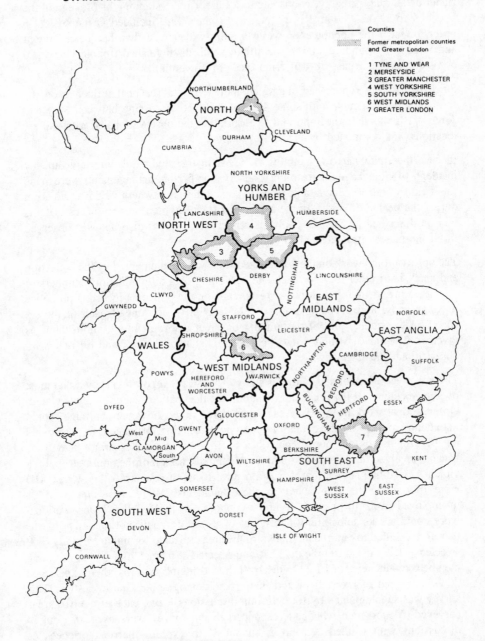

observational studies in the areas selected from the ACPO report, were intended to act as detailed case studies of the phenomenon identified, help to describe it in richer detail and, possibly, contribute to ideas for understanding or preventing the phenomenon. The "control" or "matched" sites were included in the design in order to test if the phenomenon was yet more widespread than had been thought and to see if grounds could be identified which distinguished troublesome from non-troublesome areas, thus offering clues to prevention.

Since the ACPO report had suggested there was "a seasonal influence on the frequency of incidents, with some 42% of incidents occurring between May and August", it was thought important to ensure that the observational work at all six locations was completed by the end of August.

In case the quite narrow sampling of areas in the study did not show up any incidents of violence in the fortnight's observation period, arrangements were made for stand-by staff to be available to go to some other area where violence did erupt during the period of study. In the event, this stand-by plan was not necessary. As will be described in Chapter 3 of this report, some street disorder was observed in all the major sites selected for study.

The observational work on the six selected sites was supplemented by the collection and analysis of other data for each site, including data on population, numbers of young people, drinking patterns, arrests, calls on the police as recorded on police message pads, and licensing statistics. A descriptive account of each of the six specific sites studied and of the amount of street disorder found within them, is given in Chapter 3, which draws on both this statistical work and on fieldwork observations and interviews.

There was yet a further strand to this study. The ACPO report had shown that most of the incidents (90%) causing trouble to the police were alcohol-related. Observational work in the six areas selected for study, however thorough, could not attempt to quantify the extent of young male drinking, or indeed, to put figures on the proportions of young males in a given area who either drank heavily or became involved in violence or both. Yet public discussion of the non-metropolitan violence issue had shown that it was a central focus of concern to know just who were the young men involved in these incidents. Were they employed or unemployed, well-off or poor, "yuppie yobboes" or the deprived? Observational work could tell us something of this, but of its nature could not quantify. It was therefore decided to put in hand in two of the areas selected for intensive study (one selected as having had trouble in 1987, one selected as its match) a survey of young men between the ages of 16-24 to discover their drinking patterns, their experience of violence and of the police, and their socio-demographic characteristics. This survey was supplemented by four "group discussions", two each in the two areas surveyed. Young men who had responded to the survey were asked to join in discussions with trained "group discussants" to explore their experiences of disorder and their motivation.

The results of the survey of drinking and experiences of disorder, and of the accompanying group discussions are reported in Chapter 4 of this report, which goes on to describe the kind of young man who appears to participate in street disorder and violence. Succeeding chapters of the report (Chapter 5 on drinking patterns and places of drinking; Chapter 6 on patterns of policing) present further material on how disorder incidents occur and how they might be reduced. At Chapter 7 all of this material is drawn together in a summary and final discussion.

Conclusion

The origins and outline of the research reported on in this Home Office Research Study have been described. The research reported on was set in hand rapidly and completed within four months. It relied on co-operation between the experienced staff of the Home Office Research and Planning Unit, with an already strong academic and practical background in studies of violence and of policing, and of staff in commercial market research agencies who were able to carry out at short notice the quite elaborate fieldwork and analytic tasks demanded by the research design. Although a rapid study, it was not superficial. The final chapter of this report (Chapter 7) draws together some of its more salient findings and discusses their implications for the future.

2 The locational analysis

The first task in this research was to re-analyse the 251 incidents recorded in the ACPO survey to see if more could be gleaned about the kind of areas in which they occurred. As explained at Chapter 1, the ACPO survey covered returns from the Chief Constables of England and Wales, recording incidents in the calendar year of 1987 where group violence had occurred, which needed reinforcement of ten or more officers in addition to normal sub-divisional patrol strength and where experience indicated that difficulty occurred in mobilising that level of re-inforcement in sufficient time. Only incidents taking place *outside* metropolitan areas were considered. 90% of such reported incidents were found to be alcohol-related.

The ACPO report (and the press release of June 1988) made some locational analysis of these events and remarked that many of them appeared to cluster in the most affluent counties in the South of England. It suggested that a more detailed locational analysis could be useful.

To carry out this task the Home Office Research and Planning Unit commissioned a firm of market research analysts (CACI Market Analysis Ltd), much of whose business lies in locational analysis for both commercial and public clients. Through their large existing data-base (much of it drawn from the census) CACI can map incidents, not only by their geographic location, but also by the *type* of area in which they occur. CACI have developed detailed typologies of different kinds of urban, surburban and rural areas based on census and other variables (see later and Appendix A).

Geographic clustering

Since the exact location of the 1987 reported incidents has not so far been published, it may be useful before presenting the results of the CACI analysis to present a map which shows their clustering (Map 2). They were widely spread across the country but some geographic clustering can be seen; troubled areas include coastal resorts in the West Country, Essex and North Yorkshire, a group in Suffolk another in the Thames Valley and another in Havant in Hampshire.

Incidents were most frequent in the South of England. To test this a computer analysis was made to identify a spatial "centre of gravity" for all incidents. The single place in the whole of non-metropolitan England and Wales which is in reach of most incidents was in north west Surrey. From a point just west of Camberley (the junction of the A30 and B3015), it can be estimated that 13% of all incidents are within 30 minutes average driving time; and 21% within 60 minutes driving time.

Rates of disorder by region and county

The press release issued after the ACPO report had already stated that the largest numbers of incidents reported in non-metroplitan areas were in the affluent

6

South East. Table 1, Appendix A, gives both numbers of incidents in each main "standard region" of England and Wales and rates of incidents per population in the area. The greatest numbers of incidents do indeed cluster in the affluent South East (101 of the 248 incidents it was possible to assign exactly to an area).

But the South East is the most densely populated of the standard regions. When rates of offences per total population or per population age 15-24 years are calculated (columns 2 and 3, Table 1, Appendix A), the South East is seen to be in second place behind Yorkshire and Humberside. This latter area has the greatest likelihood of disorder relative to its population density. In third place comes the South West and equal fourth are the East Midlands and East Anglia. These, like Yorkshire and Humberside, have a high rate of incidents relative to population in spite of a low absolute number of incidents. A closer look at the actual location of reported incidents in these regions showed they clustered in small pockets of disorderly places in otherwise sparsely populated areas. Coastal resorts in Yorkshire and Humberside showed clustering of incidents, as did Haverhill and Newmarket in East Anglia.

A further analysis was made at county level and gives a similar, although somewhat modified, picture. Table 2, Appendix A, gives the top ten counties in England and Wales by *rate* of incidents per size of population. Oxfordshire heads the list, followed by Berkshire, Surrey, Suffolk and North Yorkshire which is the only northern county in the "top ten" for rates of disorderly incidents.

Area classifications

The next analysis aimed to establish whether the 1987 ACPO incidents were grouped in some particular *type* of area – resort or retirement areas, areas with much local authority housing or areas defined in some other way. If this could be established, preventive strategies might be easier to devise. CACI (in conjunction with the Office of Population Censuses and Surveys) have developed a defined typology of areas which covers the whole of England and Wales. This typology of areas is given in full at Appendix A to this report. It is at two levels. The larger groupings are known as "family areas" and each "family area" includes three smaller groupings known as "cluster areas".

Each of the 1987 ACPO incidents for which there was sufficient information (all except three) were assigned firstly to the larger "family area" typology and later to the smaller, more narrowly defined, "cluster areas". Detailed results are given at Tables 3 and 4, Appendix A.

Table 3 shows that of the 248 incidents recorded by ACPO which it was possible to assign clearly to an area, only 58 were recorded from the family of "more rural areas". The majority of incidents came from the two "families" named as "higher status growth areas" (these accounted for 46 incidents) and "mixed town and country areas with some industry" (these accounted for 72 incidents). Detailed descriptions of "family" area types are given at Appendix A. The "mixed town and country" family (Family 4) is characterised by the relative importance of industry; the urban population usually exceeds the rural. The "higher status growth areas"

Map 2 Geographical distribution of serious disorder: ACPO Report 1987

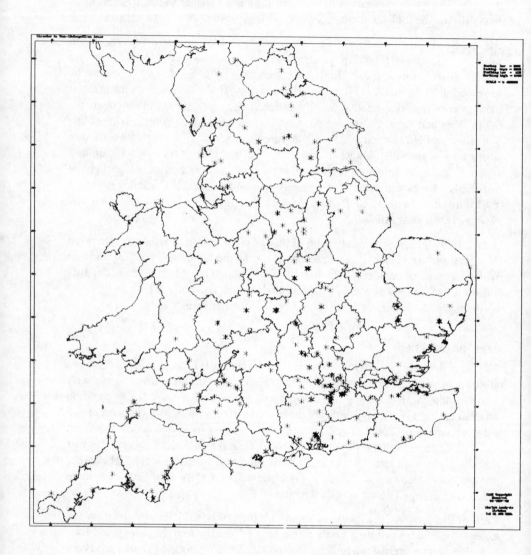

(Family 1B) are in more populated and more prosperous regions. They have a very young population with fewer over-45s and more young people than any other type of area in the United Kingdom. 118 incidents (47% of all incidents) came from these two family areas alone. They are not areas which could accurately be described as rural.

In addition to the 118 incidents from the above two families, a further 34 incidents came from cities or traditional manufacturing areas, 23 from commuting or suburban areas and 15 from seaside resort or retirement areas.

Although the absolute number of disorder incidents which came from "more rural areas" were thus only a small proportion of the total, the rates of such incidents per million of population was indeed highest in the family of "more rural areas" (Table 3, Appendix A). These showed an incident rate of 10.8 incidents per annum per million population. However, the second highest rate of disorder incidents was in "higher status growth areas".

Table 4, Appendix A, is a more refined version of Table 3, breaking down the already defined "family areas" into smaller "cluster areas". Looking particularly at the "family areas" of "mixed town and country with some industry", Table 4 shows that the largest sub-set of incidents within this wider family were in the cluster "more rural areas with industry". These provided 34 of the 72 ACPO report incidents in the "mixed town and country" family.

Arguably these incidents (in addition to the 58 incidents already classified as in the "more rural areas" family) should also be considered as "rural". However, even taking this expanded definition of "rural" incidents they still account for only 58 + 34, that is 92, of the 248 incidents recorded in the ACPO report. Thus, at the most generous estimates, only 92 out of the 248 incidents recorded by ACPO (ie 37% of all ACPO report incidents) could be considered as having taken place in "the country".

Despite the fact that the absolute number of incidents recorded by ACPO was higher in non-rural than in rural areas, Table 4 (the cluster area analysis) shows, as did Table 3 (the family area analysis), that the rates of disorder incidents per million population were higher in rural areas. Within the family of more rural areas, the highest rate of incidence was in the cluster "rural areas with transient populations". It is characteristic of these areas (see descriptive material at Appendix A) that they contain armed forces establishments within their boundaries.

Discussion

The CACI analysis supported and refined general public interpretation of the 1987 ACPO findings. The 1987 incidents recorded in the ACPO report did indeed cluster in the South of England. However, far more of them were in semi-urban than in purely rural areas. Only 58 of the 248 it was possible to assign to a given area were in the "more rural areas" family. A further 34 were in the more rural parts of the "mixed town and country with some industry" family. But nearly two thirds of the incidents recorded were in areas which could not reasonably be described as "rural".

9

Before leaving this locational analysis, a word of caution is necessary. The analysis was based on a set of incidents defined in a particular way, that given at the beginning of this chapter. It was part of the definition that incidents should be such that "experience indicated that difficulty occurred in mobilising the necessary level of reinforcement (ie of ten or more officers in addition to normal sub-divisional patrol strength) in sufficient time". Such a definition is bound to bias results towards more remote country areas. By definition it is these areas which would have most difficulty in mobilising reinforcement of more than ten policemen. Thus the fact that over a third of the ACPO 1987 set of disorder incidents were found in the more remote country is in no way surprising. Given the definition, it is perhaps more surprising that so many of them were in "mixed town and country areas with some industry" and in "high status growth areas" with denser populations and better transport facilities.

The ACPO report undoubtedly identified some problems in areas commonly described as "rural". But it cannot be taken (and was not intended to be taken) as having established that these problems were more frequent or greater than those in other non-metropolitan areas. Still less, of course, can it be taken as showing that the problems of either "rural" or "non-metropolitan" violence and disorder are a more salient problem for the police or the nation as a whole than the problems of violence or disorder within cities.

The ACPO survey was intended to establish whether a phenomenon which was thought to exist – that of violence and disorder in non-metropolitan areas where it was hard to bring up reinforcements – did indeed exist. It established the existence of that phenomenon. This further analysis shows that most of the incidents involved were not in "the country" as usually understood, but in non-rural areas.

3 Disorder in the paired towns

The second strand of this study of violence in non-metropolitan areas was to select specific sites for detailed study. It had been decided to select three sites where disorder had undoubtedly occurred in 1987 (as evidenced by the ACPO report) and to match these sites with three other, similar areas in which disorder had not been recorded by the ACPO report in 1987. This 'matched sites' design was chosen in order to discover any variations between the disorder areas and the 'control' areas which could account for the fact that disorder was seen as a problem in the former, but not the latter. Such variations could be a clue to both the causation and prevention of disorder. Another advantage of the 'matched sites' design is that it could test if the problem of disorder were even more widespread than the data captured in the ACPO report had suggested.

The three main sites for study were chosen with the help of the computer analysis recorded in the last chapter. 125 local authority districts had presented disorder problems in the ACPO report in 1987. Each of these districts was classified within a given CACI cluster and a sample of one in 5 (25) districts were then selected to represent the clusters in which they occurred. Within any given cluster the district was selected which had provided the largest number of incidents in 1987.

The next step was to use the CACI classification of all areas in England and Wales (according to the typology laid out at Appendix A) to choose the nearest matching local authority district (not mentioned on the ACPO list) to those 25 selected from the ACPO list.

From this set of 25 matched local authority districts (one with disorder recorded in 1987, one without), three pairs were then selected for further study on the following criteria:—

(i) The 'disorder' areas had to have shown the highest number of incidents within their respective clusters.

(ii) Both areas chosen within a cluster had to be reasonably representative of that cluster and hence not too dissimilar from each other.

(iii) The sites chosen had to be representative of the geographic clustering of troublesome areas within England and Wales.

The three pairs of local authority districts selected according to this procedure are listed below. The main centres of settlement within each local authority district are (where the name of the settlement differs from that of the local authority district) listed in brackets:—

11

District with disorder in 1987	Matched District without reported disorder in 1987	CACI type (see definitions Appendix A)
WOKING	GUILDFORD	Established high status *family*; commuting area *cluster*
ST EDMUNDSBURY (Haverhill)	BABERGH (Sudbury)	Mixed town and country *family*; more rural areas *cluster*
HAVANT (Cowplain)	GRAVESHAM (Gravesend)	Mixed town and country *family*; towns with surrounding country *cluster*

* Full details of the definitions and boundaries of the areas studied are given at Appendix B.

These different pairs selected cannot exemplify every type of local authority area where disorder occurs – there are no examples from the north, from seaside towns (where it is clear from the ACPO data that incidents peak at holiday seasons) or from remoter rural areas. But the spread of incidents recorded by the ACPO was too wide to cover every type of area in which they occurred. It seemed best, when only a limited number of case studies could be carried out, to concentrate on areas which were most typical and the selection of the above areas was where disorder was known to be reasonably frequent.

We thought long and hard before deciding to name the local authority districts selected for study. There are obvious difficulties. Any careful analysis of disorder in any one place can run the risk of implying that place to be particularly disorderly; and could be taken either as an insult to the citizens of that community or as a challenge to the more irresponsible among them.

For these reasons it was tempting to present the findings in anonymous fashion – describing the areas of intensive work simply as Site A, Site B and so on. Yet this option has the disadvantage of leaving results both more opaque to understanding and more difficult to challenge by future commentators and researchers. As will become clear in the following accounts, a much richer and more precise analysis is possible if specific sites are named.

Another factor affected the final decision to name specific areas. All the researchers involved in this study were impressed by the whole-hearted co-operation they received from residents of the areas studied; ranging from the young men who themselves used local pubs and clubs to the probation officers, police, licensees and others who provided interview data. These studies in concentrating on major sites of disorder within local authority areas, inevitably concentrated on major settlements within them. The citizens of Woking, Guildford, Haverhill, Sudbury,

Cowplain and Gravesend made this study possible and showed a strong desire and will to solve any problems encountered in their areas. That these particular districts were studied does not imply that they were uniquely troublesome. They were selected, in accordance with the procedure described above, simply as examples of a phenomenon which the ACPO report had already shown to be widespread.

We are confident that the citizens of these districts would themselves prefer to have access to the results of our study, without attempting to disguise its location.

Method

For each of the three pairs of towns studied, the following evidence was collated:—

(a) Background socio-demographic data about the nature of these towns, the ways in which they had changed over the years. (See Appendix C.)

(b) Data for each area drawn from available statistics about offences and licensing. (See Appendices C and F.)

(c) An analysis of all calls on the police for help with public order incidents (as recorded on police message pads) over the nine weekends in July and August 1988, over six sites. (See Appendix D.)

(d) Observational work and interviews by trained social science professionals over at least two successive weeks (and weekends) in August in each town.

A very rich data-set was thus collected for each matched pair of towns. In this preliminary report it will not be possible to present it in full.[1] In this chapter the question of how much and what kind of disorder was found in each pair of towns will be examined.

In the succeeding chapter (Chapter 4) material concerning drinking patterns in the six areas studied will be presented; in particular the results of the survey and group discussions described at page 4 above. Later chapters will draw this material together in an attempt to give some answers to the questions which gave rise to this study. But first, we will look at the simplest and most basic question: how much disorder did we find in our matched pairs of sites?

I The first pair: Haverhill and Sudbury

Background

The first pair of towns to be reported on are two smallish market towns in East Anglia; Haverhill and Sudbury. Haverhill had presented reasonably frequent incidents of disorder in 1987 in the Hayes data; Sudbury had reported none but was selected as the 'control' town. Both were within the family of areas defined as "mixed town and country".

The history of Haverhill goes back to the Middle Ages as a small country and farming community. It has never been a significantly prosperous area of Suffolk and as long as a hundred years ago was known as a centre of weekend drunkenness,

---

[1] It is hoped in due course to publish further supplementary papers on different aspects of the findings. This preliminary report will present a broad-brush picture.

where the local rural working class congregated for entertainment. In 1888, a Mr Gurteen complained to the town magistrates of disorder resulting from the consumption of alcohol taking place on the main street and at Burton End (near the present site of Haverhill Rovers Football Club). During the twenties and thirties this pattern remained unchanged. The court lists for this period show disorder offences occurring mainly at weekends and often involving youths coming into town from outlying villages. The perception of the problem grew with the increasing growth of population, especially the influx of London overspill in the sixties. Following the passing of the Town Development Act of 1952, there was established a legal agreement for the movement of people and factories to Haverhill. The industrial estate was opened in 1958 and the first new local authority housing completed a year later. The boom led not only to the importation of Londoners but also attracted people from throughout the region, particularly those looking for unskilled and semi-skilled manual jobs. Haverhill's infrastructure did not grow in parallel with its boom. It lost its rail link and the planning constraint of the bypass around the town created a corset, limiting growth of the town centre. In 1970 the policy of expansion was thrown into reverse, both by the increasing reluctance of the GLC to complete the outflows from London and, more importantly, by the growth plan for East Anglia which nominated Ipswich and Peterborough as the new growth centres. Communications were bad throughout the seventies and onwards, and consequently Haverhill has become a somewhat insular community.

Located in the Stour Valley, Sudbury is within a designated 'Area of Outstanding Natural Beauty'. An ancient market town, with roots dating back to Saxon times, Sudbury has many historic houses and churches, some built as early as the thirteenth century. Gainsborough's House, the birthplace of Thomas Gainsborough in 1727, is in the centre of the town. The town is attractive to those interested in history and art and also has a comprehensive range of sports facilities. A railway connects Sudbury to Liverpool Street, London.

There is a clear contrast between Sudbury and Haverhill. The latter has little architecture of note and few historical events for its townspeople to be proud of. Sports facilities are limited and there is no longer a railway station.

Local authority districts in which the two towns were located – Babergh (Sudbury) and St Edmundsbury (Haverhill) – had been selected as a matched pair because of similarities in their socio-demographic descriptions, especially as recorded on census data. The demography of the two towns differs from the national average in similar ways but also differs in some important ways between the two towns. Both towns have much higher proportions of young people than average in England and Wales. If comparisons are made with the national age-profile 15-19 year olds and 20-24 year olds, Haverhill has 20% more 15-19 year olds than the national rate, Sudbury 13%; Haverhill 10% more 19-24 year olds than the national rate but Sudbury only 2% more 20-24 year olds than the national norm. Both towns have also shown high rates of increase of both the absolute numbers and the proportion of young males in the population over the years 1983-1986. The change has been greater in Sudbury, where it started from a lower base.[1]

In neither town is there any appreciable ethnic minority population and the proportion in each town is similar. Rates of unemployment in both towns are similar and normal in relationship to that of Suffolk as a whole (which has a markedly low rate of unemployed compared with the rest of England and Wales). Both towns have a much higher proportion of council housing than the country as a whole, although much higher in Haverhill than Sudbury (Haverhill has just over 60% of homes classed as council houses; Sudbury a mere 36%). Both towns have relatively good housing as measured on the CACI classification by 'Acorn Group'.[2] There is little housing deprivation. Both towns have the largest proportion of their residents in the middling social classes (Registrar General's social classes 3 & 4). Sudbury has a relatively higher proportion of the higher social classes (Registrar General's 1 & 2) and a relatively lower proportion of unskilled workers.

Differences in levels of disorder

Within this study there are three different data sources for differences in levels of disorder between the two towns studied.

(a) A special analysis of Home Office statistics of Violence against the Person in each area for the years 1983-1987.

(b) An analysis of 'police message-pad' data collected in summer 1988 (see page 4 above and page 16 below).

(c) Observational data gathered by observers stationed in both towns in August 1988 (see page 4 above).

Each will be considered separately.

(a) Statistics of violence against the person

Criminal statistics available to the Home Office were analysed at small area level to produce the tables at Table 8 to 9a of Appendix C which document recorded offences of personal violence[3] in each area studied from 1983 to 1987. Too much weight cannot be given to this analysis – it is an indicator only. Both the reporting and recording of this type of offence are inevitably dubious, despite the best efforts of the police. Very often when police are called to deal with some problem of public disorder or violence they either find things are ''all quiet on arrival'' so no offence can be recorded (this itself may be a function of police response not being quickly available) or few arrests are possible due to the ratio of public to police at the event in question.

---

[1] The demographic data quoted throughout this chapter have been derived from OPCS projections using CACI modelling techniques, tables are given at Appendix C.

[2] Full details of this classification system can be obtained from CACI Market Analysis Ltd.

[3] This analysis was made on 'personal violence offences' as against 'public disorder' offences on the advice of Home Office Statistical Department.

None the less, it seemed sensible to analyse the recorded offences to see what information could be gleaned.

Table 9a, Appendix C, shows that in 1983 Haverhill had by far the largest rate of offences of violence against the person per thousand of its population, of any of the six towns studied. In 1983 Haverhill had almost three times the county rate of violence against the person, while Sudbury, by contrast, had only about a third of the same rate. These data confirm the impression recorded above that Haverhill has a greater tradition of violence that Sudbury. However, Table 9a, Appendix C (and Table 9) also show that Sudbury's rate of violent offences increased very rapidly between 1983 and 1987. It increased by an amazing 183%, while Haverhill's rate in the same period increased by a mere 17%. Thus by 1987, Haverhill had only a little more than double the rate of recorded violence against the person as had Sudbury. Recorded criminal statistics suggest that Haverhill is indeed (as the ACPO report suggested) more of a trouble-site than Sudbury.

(b) The 'police message-pad' data[1]

Because of the known difficulties of recorded statistics of violence against the person or public disorder, a decision was made to carry out an additional analysis of police message-pad data. Message pads record the stream of incidents reported to the police by members of the public, other services and police officers themselves on patrol. The reports mainly come by telephone (both 999 and ordinary lines) but some are made in person at police stations, and a few are sent over police radio. Also known as incident or occurrence sheets, message pads contain basic information such as time of receipt, name and address of complainant, nature and location of incident, initial police response (eg despatch of a patrol car) and action on the ground (eg 'youths moved on' or details of any arrest or charge).

It is known from existing research (eg Ekblom and Heal, 1982; Ramsay, 1982; Hope, 1985) that most public disorder occurs at weekends and especially on Friday and Saturday nights. The same peaking at weekends was shown in the ACPO report. Accordingly, message-pad data were examined for each of the nine weekends in July and August 1988 in each of the six areas studied, and cases of public disorder were extracted. Weekends were considered to begin at 6 am Friday and end at midnight Sunday.

The definition of public disorder used excluded (unless they happened on the street) domestic disputes, landlord/tenant disputes or any other where the setting was wholly private property. Disorder in places which were privately owned but open to the public (eg shops, stations, pubs) were included. Key words sought in message pads were 'trouble, rowdies, kids, youths, gang, yobs, noise, disturbance, fight, assault, dispute, conflict'.

As previous research has shown, message-pad analysis is a sensitive means of arriving at public perceptions of a problem, since it records demands made on the

---

[1] It is hoped to publish shortly, as an RPU paper, a fuller analysis of the police message-pad data recorded for this study.

police, even if no crime reports, arrests or actions result. The absolute number of incidents recorded in Haverhill over the nine weekends of the study was 63, in Sudbury, 51. However, the size and population of the two areas differed. Table 2, Appendix D, presents *rates* of incidents per younger male residents (aged 15-24) in each of the six areas studied. It records all incidents of public disorder, both in total and separately, for incidents involving violence (including threats) and those involving drink (mention of drunkenness, drinking or licensed premises). This gives a better, although still not perfect fix on comparative rates of disorder than a comparison not equated for size of resident population.

The table shows that calls on the police matched the assumption underlying our selection of 'disorder' towns and 'controls'. Haverhill showed far higher rates of violent incidents than Sudbury. The table further differentiates incidents recorded at the peak hour of frequency of incidents in that area (whatever time and whichever hour it occurred during the weekend, although it was almost always the hour up to midnight on a Friday or a Saturday) and the total rate of incidents per weekend. The rate of violent incidents in Haverhill in the peak pub-closing hour was the second highest found in the six areas studied and over half as high again as the rate in Sudbury: 0.19 per thousand resident male population in the 15-24 age group, versus 0.12.

The imbalance in rates of all violent incidents over the weekend as a whole (not just those recorded at peak hours) was not quite so marked. There was a rate of approximately 4.3 incidents per 1,000 15-24 year old male residents per weekend in Haverhill and 3.5 incidents per 1,000 in Sudbury.

The message-pad analysis confirmed the impression that Haverhill presents more violence and disorder than Sudbury, (both absolutely and per head of young male population) and that the difference is more marked at pub-closing time.

(c) Observational data

Originally, observation work was planned to take place in Haverhill during the first two weeks of this study (carried out in August 1988) and in Sudbury during the last two weeks. However, some reasonably substantial public order problems were witnessed in Haverhill in Week Two and so the schedule was modified slightly in order to gain maximum coverage of any further incidents. Fortunately, the two towns are within half an hour's drive of each other. The exact timing of all first-hand observations on both sites is given below.

Observations in Haverhill

During the first week of the study observers were stationed in Haverhill. Actual street and pub observations were mainly carried out at the weekend, known to be the peak time for violence or disorder (during the body of the week, fieldworkers were engaged on interview work).

Two fieldworkers carried out observations in Haverhill from 6 pm to 1 am on Friday night, 5 August 1988 and at the same hours on Saturday night, 6 August. Friday night opened slowly; the pubs were orderly, the streets quiet. During

17

opening hours a few groups of young people were seen on the street, presumably moving from pub to pub and occasionally shouting noisy greetings to each other. A lot of people seemed to know each other. But no disorder problems were observed either in pubs or on the streets during opening hours. After 11 pm and on towards 12 am, groups of youths moved to the various fish-bars and Chinese take-aways near the town centre. By this time, there were a lot of young people on the street, three quarters of them in groups of four or more. After buying food from a take-away, youngsters hung around outside talking and eating. The mood was noisy but mostly good-natured. The young people obviously did not want to go home. At 11.35 pm an incident was observed in which two groups of young men (about four in each) met head on and swore threateningly at each other. The youths were excited but it was not possible to say they were drunk. By about midnight approximately 100 people, mostly young men, were milling around the centre of Haverhill.

At about 12.05 am trouble began. About 40 more young men approached the Chinese take-away from the direction of Haverhill Rovers Football Club. At 12.15 am a mass of people from the now larger group surged across the road to an incident not visible from the observers' vantage point. The crowd by now was noisy and looked threatening. A large police van appeared several minutes later and moved cautiously into the scene. As was discovered later from the police, a Sergeant got out of his van and spoke to two people who had been assaulted by a group of six to ten others. The offending group had run off across the car park. The police van toured the car park and the surrounding area, and eventually located the group a quarter of a mile away on Camps Road. Names and addresses were taken, but the victims would not lodge an official complaint. Apparently such failure is a regular occurrence. The crowd remaining on the street dispersed slowly between 12.30 am and 1.00 am.

These incidents of Friday 5 August seem to be typical of the kind of disorder expected in the centre of Haverhill at weekends. It is to be noted that none of the behaviour witnessed resulted in charges and none of it could be laid to the account of managers of either licensed premises or food take-aways. Yet the incidents had a threatening quality for strangers in the town centre and entailed a crowd of up to 150 people, mainly young men.

On the evening of Saturday, 6 August, observers once again visited central pubs, observing street activity on foot at intervals during opening hours and then up to 12.00 am and between 12.00 am and 1.00 am, observing street activity from the car park. The evening was more cold and wet than the preceding Friday. Once again there was little trouble during opening hours. The take-aways were less busy after closing time than on Friday and between 11.00 pm and 12.00 am there were very few people on the streets. A party was going on in the Town Hall. Its music was clearly audible in the car park. One group of noisy laughing young men were gathered round a car in the car park listening to a comedy tape on the car stereo; but there was no sign of a fracas. At 12.30 am the scene outside the Chinese take-away was quiet. The party finished and two coaches arrived outside the Town Hall, presumably to take guests home. Other guests left on foot and by car. The young people, of whom there were a fair number, were mostly drunken and noisy but not aggressive or threatening. They were in high spirits and sounded and looked as if they'd had a good time.

Throughout the period after closing time, police patrols were more noticeable than the previous evening, but not obtrusive. By 1.00 am the town was quiet.

On the Thursday following the first weekend observers again spent time visiting pubs and take-aways and checking streets between 6.00 pm and 12.30 am. The Thursday evening was wet, there were few people on the streets and the take-aways were doing little business. No trouble was observed.

The second Friday night observation in Haverhill was on 12 August 1988. It was a dry, warm evening. One of the night-clubs in the town was visited. There was no sign of any violent incidents either inside or outside the club. Once again, trouble seemed only to come after closing time. The following account was written by one of the fieldworkers immediately after the event.

"Drove into town at 11.30 pm. Observed approximately 30 people outside the Wimpy Bar (Benny's had now shut for holidays). We parked the car and walked up the Camps Road to the Black Horse pub. No sign of any activity. Walked back to the Wimpy to buy some food (11.50 pm). There were two groups of young men (about 20) still waiting for food. They were very drunk and using obscene language. They walked up towards the Hamlet Road end of town in front of us. We walked slowly up though town, observing a gathering at the taxi rank (mixed sex, about 20 people); a lot of people on the streets. On reaching the Chinese take-away, we saw a group of about 50 people outside; the Chinese itself being full with people waiting for food. We returned to the car to observe the scene.

Throughout this period (from 11.30 pm to 12.15 am) we noted an increased police presence. A vehicle was stationed outside Blushes (a local night-club) and there were three pairs of policemen and women, standing in inconspicuous spots, watching the gatherings. Police vehicles were seen at regular intervals driving through town.

At 12.15 am there was a loud noise and shouting coming from the Hamlet Road direction, and people ran from the Chinese towards the noise. We left the car and walked quickly in the same direction. As we rounded the corner into Hamlet Road we were confronted with a group of approximately 200 people moving towards us. The nucleus of the group was on the left hand side of the road, and was all-male, and all young looking. The noise was coming from this group. It was decided by one member of the team that the situation was too dangerous to walk into, so we turned round and returned to the car.

The group walked up to the Chinese take-away and re-gathered outside the Job Centre. At this point the large police van arrived. There was a minor scuffle in the middle of the group, which died down when two PCs walked over and began to talk to the young people. There were four or five small groups observing the scene. A total of five police officers, two WPCs and three PCs

19

mingled with the crowd for 15 minutes and appeared to be diffusing what looked to be a potentially hazardous situation. They herded the group towards the town centre. The mass divided into smaller groups and some made their way home. Two remaining large groups were herded towards the Wimpy and the Pightle, with one police officer on each side of the road, walking slowly behind them. This took another 15 minutes, and involved a lot of jeering and baiting of the police officers.

The young people congregated, one group on the corner of Queen Street and the Pightle, the other outside St Mary's Church on the Camps Road. They then moved back up town, towards the Chinese take-away, again with the police walking slowly behind and taking a lot of verbal abuse. Police vehicles were stationed at points on the High Street, never far from the groups. Both groups lingered at the White Hart for about 10 minutes, then split, and made their way home, still followed by police vehicles.

We discovered by talking to the police later, that the large group had come from Haverhill Rovers Football Club after a disco. There had been an incident outside the club, which is in Hamlet Road, hence the large gathering.''

By now the fieldworkers had observed two successive troublesome Friday nights in Haverhill. They were anxious not to become too easily recognised and decided to visit Sudbury the following night, Saturday, 13 August (see below). They did, however, return to Haverhill for another Saturday evening's observation on Saturday 20 August. It was a rainy wet night, the streets were quiet and there were no signs of trouble.

During the third week of their study, fieldworkers picked up some rumours that Haverhill could be the scene of trouble on the evening of Friday 26 August – it was said that local youths planned to attack the police. So although early evening of Friday 26 August was spent in Sudbury (see below), the fieldworkers drove in to Haverhill after closing time. It was a fairly wet cold evening. In the event, no serious trouble took place, but the following fieldwork notes give a flavour of the evening.

"Arrived in Haverhill at 11.20 pm just as the pubs were emptying out. Drove around town once and observed a lot of people on the streets. There were many small groups, ie 2/3/4 and one large group (about 25) outside the Wimpy.

Larger proportions of women than the last Friday night.

Parked the car in the Provincial car park. Large police van appeared and toured the car park. About nine police constables inside the van. We had also observed four foot patrol constables, making 13 in all.

We walked to the Wimpy, where there was now a smaller gathering of about 12 people, all male. One little group of five males, age 17-20, made fun of everyone walking past, including us, calling one of us a 'Jeremy'!

We walked back to the car park. People were now beginning to go home (midnight). On reaching the car park we heard loud screaming and shouting coming from Duddery Hill. We walked round to see that the large police van had arrived, and two PCs were dealing with the incident, which was quite a fierce domestic. The man and woman involved were in night-clothes and clearly distressed.

The incident died down quietly, we drove around the town until 1.30 am, but all was quiet, with only a few stragglers left on the streets.''

This was a reasonably peaceful evening for Haverhill, although not without some problems.

Some final observations were made in Haverhill, late at night on Sunday 28 August. Since the following day was a Bank Holiday, it had been suggested that there might be trouble. Observers once again arrived in Haverhill at 11.20 pm and recorded the following.

"People leaving pubs mainly in pairs. Some groups of up to half a dozen. Gathering at the Wimpy – friendly but noisy. Gradually dispersed. Police presence unseen until about 12.15 am. Two on foot plus one patrol car. No incidents.''

Observations in Sudbury

The first pub and street observations in Sudbury were made on the evening of Saturday 13 August, between 7.00 pm and 12.00 am. (The observers felt they had been noticed in Haverhill the night before and should move on to Sudbury.) That Saturday night in Sudbury was very calm. Dispersal from pubs after closing time was quick in relation to Haverhill, and quiet. A police patrol car was seen twice in the hour after closing time the observers spent walking round the town. No foot patrols were seen. The fast-food outlets attracted custom from the pubs, but there were no large gatherings and people dispersed shortly after purchasing their food.

Further observations were made in Sudbury on a Friday night (19 August) a week later. Once again, no problems were observed and people dispersed peacefully at closing time. Such gatherings as there were at fast-food outlets were non-aggressive and dispersed rapidly.

The early part of the evening of Friday 26 August observers were also in Sudbury (although at 11.00 pm they drove to Haverhill; see above). No serious trouble was observed. The evening of Saturday 27 August was also spent in Sudbury. Observers went on from their pub visits to a night-club which closed at 2.00 am. A large group gathered outside in the car park after closing but dispersed without undue noise or incident. There was no trouble to speak of and very little sign of the police during the evening. Their presence was apparent when the observers returned to the town centre at 2.20 am. Two were seen on foot, two cars and one van. They appeared to be checking the main streets after closure of the two discos operating that night. Observers returned to their hotel at 3.00 am having seen no trouble.

Sudbury was again observed on Sunday evening, 28 August up to 11.00 pm and on Bank Holiday Monday 29 August. On neither occasion was trouble observed. On both evenings people dispersed quietly after closing time leaving the streets quiet.

21

Summary of data on Sudbury and Haverhill

The above observations suggest that Haverhill is indeed a town which has frequent closing-time public order problems of the sort documented in the ACPO report; and that Sudbury, the 'control' town, is much freer of such incidents.

The same picture emerged from the analyses of statistics of violence against the person and of police message-pad data.

II The second pair: Woking and Guildford

Background

The second pair of towns studied was Woking and Guildford. Incidents in Woking figured largely in the ACPO 1987 data. Guildford had reported no disorder incidents of the ACPO type in 1987 and was selected as the 'control' town, by the method described at page 11 above. Both were within the family of areas defined as 'established high-status areas'.

The police sub-division in which Woking lies was described to our researchers as "wall to wall brick". The separate villages of Old Woking, St Johns, Sheerwater and West Byfleet have all joined together to produce a straggling semi-conurbation. The town centre is a small one, mainly dedicated to shops and offices. There is a library and a swimming pool, both due to be modernised. The shopping centre is also in the process of being modernised and has been described, somewhat unkindly, by the local paper as 'a shambles'.

Woking is not a glamorous place. None the less, it has long been an entertainment and drinking centre. Woking station is an important interchange on the railway network, especially for the military based in the Aldershot-Woking-Guildford area. It has a late night train service which means that a large number of different groups congregate at the railway station late at night to take the last trains home. The railway station has something of a history of violence and, in the past, has sometimes had to be closed on a Friday or Saturday night.

Guildford, by contrast, is a town which has developed outward from an ancient historic centre. The central area consists of High Street and North Street. High Street is cobbled and flanked with a mixture of historic and modern buildings, up-market shops and chainstores. North Street has more modern buildings, is also a mixture of shops and offices and leads to the large Friary shopping precinct and bus station. Guildford is well served by transport. There are good bus connections with the rest of Surrey and into Hampshire and good train connections to London, the south coast and nearby Woking. The rail service linking Guildford with Woking, Aldershot and Pirbright, is much used by young people coming into Guildford for an evening's entertainment.

The two areas had been paired because of overall similarities in their socio-demographic descriptions, but once again (as with Haverhill and Sudbury) there were some important differences. The proportion of 15-19 year olds in both towns is near to both the Surrey and national averages. Woking, however, has 10% more

20-24 year olds than the average rate for Surrey, while the proportion of 20-24 year olds in Guildford is close to the Surrey norm, which is itself lower than the normal rate for England and Wales as a whole (see tables at Appendix C).

Looking historically at *changes* in the population of young people in both towns, there has been an increase in the absolute number of 20-24 year old young males in Woking of 20% over the years between 1981 and 1986. During the same period the absolute number of 20-24 year olds in Guildford has fallen by 4%. Similar changes are recorded if one looks at the ratio of young men to the total population in both towns. These population changes are likely to have caused more stress in Woking than Guildford.

Woking has a relatively high proportion of residents from the Indian sub-continent compared to the rest of Surrey or England and Wales, but those born in the Indian sub-continent still account for less than 2% of the total population. The size of ethnic minority populations in Guildford is around the national average.

The unemployment rate in both towns is low by national comparisons, although slightly higher in Guildford than Woking. In Woking 21% of dwellings are council houses, in Guildford 28%. Both towns have relatively affluent housing compared to national norms. Perhaps surprisingly Woking has a greater proportion of housing classified as affluent (62%) than has Guildford (44%).

Woking and Guildford are two similar prosperous Surrey towns with comparatively low unemployment and good housing. Guildford has more of a historic centre; but Woking appears to have the edge in housing affluence. Both towns have high and rapidly growing young male populations, but the proportion of young males in Woking is higher and has grown more rapidly.

Difference in levels of disorder

As in the discussion of Haverhill and Sudbury, the evidence here will be considered under three headings:—

(a) Evidence from statistics of violence against the person from 1983-1987.

(b) Evidence from police message-pad data collected in summer 1988.

(c) Observational data gathered in August 1988.

(a) Statistics of violence against the person

Table 9a, Appendix C, shows that in 1983 Guildford had a higher rate of recorded offences of violence against the person than did Woking (six offences recorded per thousand of male population as against four per thousand in Woking). By 1987 this gap had narrowed, with Guildford showing just over seven offences per thousand of male population and Woking just under seven offences. Woking's rate of violence against the person was increasing during these years at a far faster rate than Guildford's, a point possibly connected with the similar growth in Woking's young male population over these years, while that in Guildford fell. These data suggest that at the time of the study, rates of violence did not vary greatly between the two towns.

23

(b) Police message-pad data

Over the nine weekends of the study, 89 incidents of public disorder of all types were recorded in Woking, 90 in Guildford. However, as for Haverhill and Sudbury, it is necessary to calculate rates of incidents per size of population in order to make sensible comparisons. On weekend rates of violent disorder incidents per thousand of the young male population aged 15-24 (Table 2, Appendix D) Woking had 0.61 such offences as against Guildford's 0.82. With the rates for the peak hour, Woking had 0.11, Guildford 0.12. If anything, it is Guildford, the 'control' town, which has a higher rate of violent disorder incidents than Woking, the selected 'trouble town'.

(c) Observational data

As in Haverhill and Sudbury, fieldworkers concentrated their observational work over the weekends.

Observations in Woking

The first weekend of Woking fieldwork was from Thursday to Saturday, 4-6 August 1988 and the second weekend was from 11-13 August. Observers visited many different pubs, discos, night-clubs, wandered the streets, observed take-away fast-food places after closing time and stayed on the streets until all was quiet.

They observed nothing parallel to the Haverhill street scenes previously described. Woking pubs and take-away joints could be noisy – but dispersal was peaceful. None the less, public order incidents were occurring here and there across the area which the fieldworkers did not themselves directly observe but which were reported to them later by the police. On one Saturday night there was a brief flare of trouble at a kebab van. A drunk getting awkward led to two arrests being made. Because the incident had been witnessed by a crowd of people round the van, the police remained on the scene until the groups had drifted away from the kebab van and nearby taxi rank. By 12.30 am most people had left. Another incident occurred at McDonalds on a Saturday night. Three people using McDonalds, one of whom was very drunk and abusive to other customers, were ejected by the bouncer. The drunken customer tried to force his way back in at which point the McDonalds Duty Manager called the police. As the police were arresting the offender his two companions objected which led to three arrests.

The police suggested these incidents were fairly typical of Woking weekend trouble in 1988. However, they made a further important point, Woking had been the scene of extensive central area problems in 1987 (the year in which the ACPO data were collected). Police were then suffering from excessive baiting from young people gathering in the central area around the shopping centre. Special police efforts were made and within the last 12 months, the size of groups involved in the street in public order problems had, according to police estimates, been reduced from two hundred plus to thirty plus.

Two reasons were advanced for this improvement in Woking's public order problem. Two particular places of late night entertainment had been thought to be attracting a particularly difficult crowd, arriving in Woking 'looking for trouble'. Both were thought to have been suffering from bad management and had since been closed. The police had also introduced a policy that no officer must threaten to arrest without carrying the arrest through, and believe this policy had helped. Our observers were also told that it is now the tactic of police in Woking not to accept any form of verbal abuse. This is seen as an unacceptable form of behaviour not to be tolerated by the police on duty.

Observations in Guildford

The study of Guildford was carried out in the last two weeks of August. Weekend observations were carried out on two successive Friday, Saturday and Sunday nights August 19-21 and 26-28. As in other towns, they included detailed in-premises observations together with a 'beat' in the locality of the entertainment facilities. This was followed by observations after pub-closing time until the areas were quiet (in the region of 90 minutes).

The Guildford fieldworkers themselves wrote the following summary description of their observations. It is worth quoting in full as a vivid description of a busy although not particularly troublesome social life over the weekend in a provincial centre of entertainment.

"Friday and Saturday Night

Central area of Guildford quiet between shop closing and 7.30-8.00 pm. There is a small overlap especially at the Three Pigeons between business/shopping trade and people out for the night in the 20+ age range. By 8 pm the young are arriving from the train/bus station area of town – some heading directly to the three-screen cinema at the north eastern end of the High Street. The majority start their evening in the Blackfriars, positioned under the shopping precinct; then they may either congregate outside the Wimpy on the opposite corner to the Blackfriars or go inside to eat. They move up to North Street – sometimes in groups of 10+ towards the Mary Rose in Leapale Street, some go into the Elevens Bar, others move on to the Horse and Groom.

During the course of the evening there is a steady movement up and down North Street, sometimes in groups divided in threes/fours to walk along the pavement.

People are usually settled by 10.15 pm. There is also a movement of cinema-goers – some young girls looking quite nervous – heading in the direction of the train/bus station. There was some other movement by some people about 10.45 pm from the Horse and Groom – that shuts promptly and sometimes just before the other pubs – to the Blackfriars for a more leisurely last drink.

Although the Wimpy is temporarily shutting at 11 pm to try and stop congregation/trouble outside its premises, people still gather there and talk/push and shove/play fight; mixture 60% male to 40% female.

There is a gradual drift away either to walk north west out of the centre or to the taxi rank to wait for a taxi home – this can result in another half an hour of congregation. Some cars and motor-bikes cruising the area.

25

Since the Wimpy has shut there is some movement to the Kebab shop in Market Street or the Kentucky Fried Chicken in the upper High Street area. Some movement by older youths to the Indian Restaurant in North Street above shops on corner of Market Street. The entrance to Cinderella's at the top end of North Street is busy with people trying to get in between 11 pm and 11.30 pm. Some movement up to Cinderella's Night Club. 2 am smooth dispersal of people by car and taxi.

Sunday Night

Very similar pattern to Friday and Saturday except greater numbers of 15+ age group arriving in town 8 pm for Cinderella's Juice Disco. Some walking up North Street from train/bus station – others walking down High Street (from Merrow direction) – more low horse power motor bikes on roads than on Friday/Saturday nights. When Juice Disco shuts some dispersal down North Street to stations, some walking to upper end of High Street – McDonalds and buses for Merrow, few collected by parents from outside disco.

Dispersal of town complete by 11.30 pm on Sunday – pubs shutting at 10.30 pm. Small congregation of motor bikes outside McDonalds.

Central area defined by whole of North Street and corner of Onslow Street centred on three main pubs, a bar and a fast-food outlet, Wimpy. People start at the lower end of North Street with the Blackfriars pub and then some will eat in the Wimpy and Pizza Hut – 8.30-9 pm. Alternatively, people will move into the Mary Rose and/or Elevens Bar settling in the Horse and Groom around 10 pm – some of whom will return to the Blackfriars for a final drink – this may be because the Horse and Groom closes a few minutes before regular closing hours.

At closing time the majority of movement is down North Street towards the Wimpy Bar, taxi rank and stations. On Sunday evenings at 10 pm, the 'Juice Disco' finishes at Cinderella's and there is a movement up towards McDonalds of pedestrians and motor-cyclists.''

The above is the fieldworkers' general description of movements in Guildford town centre over the weekend. During the two weekends of fieldwork, two specific incidents of disorder were observed.

The first was at about 10.00 pm on Saturday 20 August. A woman outside a pub in the central district complained noisily that her brother was being hunted by a large group in retaliation for a fight the preceding night. About twenty people in a group indeed appeared to be going in and out of nearby pubs looking for someone. The group was finally dispersed when police attached to a nearby Personnel Carrier joined the scene. Most of the police stood back, but one (a dog-handler) moved over to the group and dispersed them.

The second incident was on Market Street at about 10.15 pm on Friday 26 August. Observers saw a fight between 12 to 13 youths in two groups – one slightly younger, one slightly older. The fighting was fairly rough but ended for no apparent reason when the older group moved off. When the younger group were

26

asked what had happened, they replied "no reason – that is Guildford on a Friday night". The younger group flagged down a police car in the street to report the incident. Police told them they would contact them if they found the attackers. Two of the younger group went home. The others suggested to the fieldworkers that the incident had occurred because they did not fit in to the bar and had been ridiculed because they said thank you to the bar staff. (This incident was not included on police records.)

It should be noted that during the two-week period of fieldwork in Guildford, 'Block Leave' was in operation at the barracks of Aldershot and Pirbright. This led to greatly reduced numbers of soldiers having access to the town at this time. Several interviewees suggested to the fieldworkers that this had caused a particularly quiet time in Guildford. "Squaddies" are very commonly perceived as the source of much disorder.

Summary of observations on Woking and Guildford

Despite the fact that Woking had been selected for a case study of a trouble-site, and Guildford as a control, the actual level of problems did not differ much between the two areas; indeed, the police message-pad data suggests that in July and August 1988, Guildford was experiencing more incidents of disorder than Woking. Interview data (both with the police and others) suggested that Woking had experienced quite serious street disorder problems in 1987 but agreed that things were much improved in 1988.

In the summer of 1988, both towns appeared to be experiencing their fair share of the type of minor disorder incidents associated with any entertainment area (compare, for instance, Ramsay 1982 on entertainment centre violence in Southampton) but not to present (at least on the weekends observed) the kind of street mob trouble which was witnessed in Haverhill.

III The third pair: Cowplain and Gravesham

The third pair of sites studied was Cowplain and Gravesham. Both are within the family of areas described as "mixed town and country areas with some industry". Within this general area-type they fall into the sub-group of "more industrial areas". Many incidents of non-metropolitan violence stemmed from this type of area. Cowplain was the scene of considerable disorder in 1987, as recorded in the ACPO report. Gravesham was selected as a matching area by the CACI computer analysis.

Background

Cowplain differs from the other areas studied in this project in that it cannot be described as a 'town' – even a small one. It does not have a natural centre but is part of a rambling, difficult to delimit, suburban-cum-rural sprawl lying to the north and west of Portsmouth.

The first impression of any visitor to the Cowplain area is of an attractive, orderly residential environment. There is a lot of excellent housing, many pretty gardens

27

and few signs of litter. It seems a preferable and pretty part of the world; not a place where violence and disorder would be expected.

In order to give focus to their study, the observers spend much of their first few days driving around and talking to local residents, youth-workers, transport workers and police in order to identify sites where young people gathered and the circuits used by them.

The most obvious target for attention was the *Waterlooville Centre* and its surrounding entertainment outlets. It is the nearest in the neighbourhood to an identifiable centre and its shopping precinct is a natural focus which the police perceive as a possible area of conflict and disorder. The area attracts a wide range of people, cutting across social class.

Another area or circuit selected for closer observation was the group of streets and pubs close to the *Wecock Farm* housing estate. Connected to, but at a slight distance from the immediate Wecock Farm area is the *Horndean and North Cowplain* circuit. This area was selected for attention mainly from information gathered from cab drivers and the police. There was said to be much coming and going between the Horndean and North Cowplain group of pubs and those in the Wecock Farm area.

These three sub-areas within the general area of Cowplain became the focus of observational work.

Gravesham, the site selected by the computer analysis as a 'match' or 'control' for Cowplain, has the same sort of mix of housing, rural areas and light industry. It too is "mixed town and country with some industry". But where Cowplain lies to the outskirts of a large town (Portsmouth), Gravesham has its own natural centre within it, the town of Gravesend. The whole area of Gravesham consists of seven parishes: Gravesend, Northfleet, Cobham, Higham, Luddesdown, Meopham and Shorne. Gravesend and Northfleet contain 80% of the population. Many remaining parishes are picturesque villages.

Like Cowplain, the Gravesham area appears immediately to the casual visitor as pleasant, affluent and well-kept; by no means a natural site of violence or disorder. The beauty of the countryside attracts some tourism to parts of the area. Preliminary interviews and observations suggested that Gravesend itself was the main centre of entertainment for the area and the magnet and focus of any disorder. It is a historic town with some pleasant buildings, its culture traditionally connected with the river and the docks. Tilbury is just across the water and Chatham only a few miles away.

Both Cowplain and Gravesham have proportions of young people and young males in their population, fairly similar to the proportion normal for their counties or for England and Wales as a whole (see tables at Appendix C). Gravesham, however, has a slightly larger proportion of both young males aged 15-19 and young males aged 20-24 than does Cowplain, although the difference is not marked.

Cowplain, however, has seen an exceptionally rapid rate of increase in its young male population over the years from 1981-1986. Table 2a (Appendix C) shows that the number of males in the 20-24 age group has risen by 40% in proportion to the general population of the area, over these five years. There was a similar rise in the proportion of the population in this age group in Gravesend (a 10% change) but nothing like so marked. As was suggested at page 23 above, rapid change in the proportions of young males in an area can cause stress.

There are few ethnic minorities in the Cowplain area; Gravesend has a more ethnically mixed population with a substantial long-settled Sikh community. Cowplain has a current unemployment rate marginally above that to be expected for the county of Hampshire, but much lower than that for England and Wales as a whole. Gravesham, however, has an unemployment rate 64% higher than could be expected for Kent as a whole and even 14% higher than the national figures for England and Wales. In both areas, unemployment has been dropping rapidly; in Cowplain at a rate 13% faster than for Hampshire as a whole, in Gravesham at a rate 30% faster than for Kent as a whole.

Cowplain has by and large very affluent housing (70% of the housing in the area falls into this classification) and has a very low level of council housing. But a third of the council housing which does exist is classified as 'poor'. It is thus an area of great polarity of housing stock – mainly wealthy, but with pockets of poorer council housing. Gravesham, by contrast, is more even in its distribution of housing stock. It has more council housing than to be expected in Kent but a lower proportion than would be expected for England and Wales as a whole. The social class data for the two towns gives the same picture as the housing data. Cowplain is more polarised, nearly 60% of its workers being in the top two social classes, but has a substantial minority of semi and unskilled workers. The class distribution of workers in Gravesham is nearer to the norm.

Differences in levels of disorder

Once again, three different data-sets will be presented to describe levels of disorder in the two paired areas:—

(a) Statistics of violence against the person 1983-1987.

(b) The 'police message-pad' data collected in summer 1988.

(c) The observational data collected in August 1988.

(a) Statistics of violence against the person

Table 9a, Appendix C, shows that both Cowplain and Gravesham showed high rates of violence against the person offences in 1987. The rates were about the same as for Haverhill (a trouble-site) in *both* areas in this pair; 12.8 offences per thousand of male population in Cowplain, 12.4 offences per thousand of male population in Gravesham (Haverhill had shown a rate of 12.5 per thousand of male population in 1987). The Cowplain rate had risen from a lower base in 1983 (6.3 offences per thousand male population) than had the Gravesham rate. In 1983 Gravesham already had a rate of 9.2 violence against the person offences per thousand of the population. The more rapid rise in Cowplain's young male population (see page 29 above) may be connected with this more rapid rate of change.

(b) The 'police message-pad' data

The methodology of the message-pad analysis has been described at page 16 above. Over the nine weekends of the study in Cowplain and Gravesend in July and August 1988, 57 incidents were recorded in Cowplain and 97 in Gravesend. To make a more valid comparison of the extent of disorder on each site during these nine weeks, it was necessary to translate these raw figures into rates of disorder incidents per thousand of the population. Table 2, Appendix D, shows that Cowplain rates were only marginally worse than those found in Gravesend. For instance, Cowplain showed 1.6 violent disorder incidents per weekend per thousand of the male population aged 15-24, Gravesend 1.4 such incidents. When similar calculations were made for the peak hour of violence (usually immediately after closing time on Friday or Saturday; see pages 17 and 24), Cowplain showed 0.45 such incidents per thousand of the male population aged 15-24 and Gravesend 0.17 such incidents. The 1987 'trouble-site' is showing more incidents on this message-pad data analysis; but the 'control' site – Gravesham – ranks third out of the six towns studied (close behind Haverhill) when population rates are considered. In absolute terms, Gravesend had the highest rate of violent disorder incidents of all six towns – 5 per weekend, as Table 1, Appendix D shows.

(c) Observational data

As in the other paired towns, fieldworkers concentrated their direct observational work over the weekends in August 1988, spreading their time between the two towns.

Observations in Cowplain

As explained at page 27 above, there was no single natural centre of likely disorder and violence in Cowplain. Three possible circuit or target areas were identified by fieldworkers in the first few days – the Waterlooville Centre and its immediate environs, the neighbourhood of the Wecock Farm housing estate and the area the researchers named as Horndean or North Cowplain.

Observations started on Friday 5 August 1988 around the Waterlooville Centre. (The following account is summarised from fieldworker observations.) It was a warm and pleasant evening and observers split their time between the neighbouring pubs, and strolling round the shopping precinct. It was a busy evening with many intermingling groups of youths, many of whom knew each other well. Quite early in the evening there was a lot of symbolic violence (mock fights and abuse) and horseplay by the younger groups. A core group of youths wandered to and fro between the three main pubs in the vicinity. The central actor carried a glass of barley wine, the others cans, one of which was Coca-Cola. They looked about 17. About 10 pm a police patrol car arrived at one pub to investigate a brawl, but this had dispersed when they arrived. During the next hour the observers heard groups of youths complaining about 'The Wecocks' (ie lads from the Wecock Farm estate a little to the north. One young man had injured his arm in a fracas with them that evening.

Police patrolled the area throughout the evening by foot and in the personnel carrier. As pubs closed, groups of young people of both sexes meandered down to the fish and chip shop. The groups were recognisable from earlier in the evening. They mingled with each other. One group of both sexes was rather rowdy. The police watched them and as the noisiest member turned down a side road they followed. He was cornered by the PCs. He then made more noise than ever and seemed to be blaming 'The Wecocks'. He walked away with the PCs who 'decided not to arrest him' but took him to hospital where he was treated for a broken wrist.

The night ended quietly with youngsters buying chips which they ate on their way home. No one from the young groups used the taxi service. The older age group present dispersed more quickly when the pubs closed. When they did meet the young they exchanged friendly greetings. The observers found the atmosphere of the whole evening informal and not threatening – but there was the latent sense of hostility to 'the Wecocks' and there had been isolated instances of disorder.

The following night, Saturday 6 August, was again fine and warm. Observers used it to reconnoitre thoroughly the Horndean and North Cowplain area. Some pubs in this area act as home base for small groups of regular drinkers often of mixed age groups. Others are large busy youth pubs with a clientele age about 16-30, attracting 400 or so people on Saturday night. The 'Red Lion' seems to be a magnet attracting a great deal of trade from all over the area. It does not appear to attract disorder or generate it. Although crowded and busy it is a place where people meet and the norm of behaviour is pleasant and sociable. At the exit to the pub, people spill out into the area outside, laid out with tables, chairs and potted plants. There is a busy Indian restaurant next door.

As the area emptied, taxis took people off in various directions. The observers walked over to Cowplain and the Kentucky Fried Chicken after pub-closing time. A few young men were eating there. By midnight the whole area was quiet and deserted.

Weekend observations began again on Friday 12 August. From 6 pm to 8.30 pm they toured all three areas (Waterlooville, Wecock Farm and North Cowplain). One observer left his bicycle chained to the rack in Waterlooville shopping precinct where it remained safe all night. From 8.30 pm to about 9.30 pm time was spent in the Red Lion, the busy 'magnet' pub in North Cowplain. A group of young men were spotted drinking there who stood around together looking menacing. This behaviour is not usual in the Red Lion. They then marched through the length of the pub in a determined way (most people smile and chat as they pass through these crowds). On leaving the pub the observers saw the same group of young men striding purposefully through the streets. They followed them to one of the smaller pubs, catering for regulars of Horndean and North Cowplain. It was a working-class pub with darts board, fruit machine and juke box. When the observers entered this pub the atmosphere was very tense. The 'invading' group

31

sat on one side of the room in one corner, and the regulars sat on the opposite side of the room. Two women walked past the 'invaders' and they made insulting comments to the younger woman. She was distressed and the local men were angry. The older woman tried to calm the locals down and took the 'invaders' to task. Tension rose. While she was talking, the 'invaders' were stacking empty bottles under the table. Three of the group left the table and convened outside the pub. They returned singly and the invader group began lining up the bottles they had hidden under the table. Suddenly both groups (locals and invaders) rushed outside into the car park. Observers followed and joined some local men just outside. One man mentioned 'Wecock' and said that he thought this a retaliation attack. The women screamed and the men taunted each other. The women physically held the men apart. Each group was a few yards from each other. One man gave a loud cry and someone threw a bottle which crashed through the windows of a taxi. As this happened the crowd of about 30-40 became silent, then a babble of noise broke out. From the conversation it seemed as if this last action was not acceptable behaviour. No one attempted to continue the conflict and the 'intruders' disappeared.

The personnel carrier with about 12 policemen arrived quietly, but one PC defused the situation. He seemed on friendly terms with the crowd (about 20 people now, as many had returned inside or disappeared).

The observers entered the pub and spoke to the landlord. He acted as if nothing had happened. Maybe he saw nothing; the pub doors were closed as soon as the rumpus started.

The incident was territorial and did not seem to be drink-related. There seemed to be an unwritten code of 'no real violence'. It was a symbolic conflict. Some of the people in the pub joined the 'invaders' outside. Were those people already planted and waiting in the pub? Later in the week the observers saw one such youth playing pool in a pub on the Wecock estate.

After this incident (at 11 pm) the observers returned to the Red Lion to observe the peaceful dispersal of drinkers; checked a pizza take-away and Indian restaurant which were peaceful, and at 11.45 pm concluded by driving round the whole observation area, finding it deserted except for one or two people walking home.

The next observations were on the evening of Saturday 13 August. The weather was colder than on other observation days. Observations centred on the Waterlooville precinct area. The tone of the evening was quite calm and although the observable age group was under 25, the over 20s were more evident than they had been last weekend.

In one pub, groups of young men and young women discussed the evening's activities, and it seemed as if they intended to travel as single sex groups; but at the end of the evening there were many in couples.

In another pub a party celebrated the wedding of a local Hell's Angel. The music rivalled that of a neighbouring place where another party was under way. Very few people were in the precinct and the evening passed quietly. At closing time the beat policemen chatted companionably with passing young people and all age groups headed for the take-aways.

This was the busiest the observers had seen the Chinese take-away with about eight people queueing. Their ages were between 28 and 80. The fish and chip shop opposite had a younger clientele. That night there was congestion around the fish and chip shop and the taxi rank, but the disorder here was caused by the man of about 80 who was drunk. The last people the observers saw in the precinct were two in their 50s, well-dressed and window shopping. This was 12.05 am.

Observations in Gravesham

During the first week of the study in Gravesham, observers drove round the whole area and carried out many interviews with the police and local people. As a result of this preliminary work it was quite clear that the major trouble site in the Gravesham area was the Gravesend town centre, which acted as a magnet for the whole area around. Observations tended to confirm the stories that prescribed Gravesend town centre as a backdrop to youthful disorder and mayhem. It was decided to concentrate on this tight area of public houses, restaurants and fast-food outlets. At weekends the streets running through this area are alive with a party spirit as 'kids' move from one premises to another.

The first weekend's observation (Friday to Sunday, 19-21 August) took in streets in the centre including pedestrianised streets, as many as 15 different pubs or places of drinking, the McDonalds take-away in the centre, an array of other take-away eating places, the taxi rank off the top of Windmill Street and the late night petrol station on King Street.

So much action was observed that it is difficult to summarise. Observers were able to categorise different groups of young people wandering about and centering on different pubs. They christened the different groups Circuit Group 1, 2, 3 and 4. Group 1 was essentially male and working class. Members went about in gangs and they age range was about 16-28. Behaviour style was aggressive and confrontational. They tended to dress in cheap, less fashionable clothing, to talk violently, to drink heavily and be at the centre of disorder incidents. Group 2 was again mainly male, but in terms of dress and style was more 'top man' high-street fashion reflecting mass youth cultural tastes. The group was far more likely than Group 1 to be in mixed sex groups. The behaviour of this group, whilst often rowdy, would typically consist of shouting at other people in the street, or between themselves, or walking along the street in a line singing. It was less overtly confrontational than the behaviour of Group 1. Group 3 were, on average, slightly older, tended to wear even more expensive up-market clothes and move in smaller mixed sex groups. They were identified by the others as 'posers'. Their behaviour was distinctly non-aggressive without the same gratuitous drinking as other groups. They tended to mix races more easily and frequently than the other groups. Group 4 were at the older end of the target group. They were about 60% male and 40% female. Some of the venues they used had customers of age 40+, although still ostensibly young drinking places. They included elements from a wider set of youth sub-cultures, including the odd 'Goth', a weekend punk, social and community workers. This group was the least loud and aggressive.

33

All four circuit groups had their own identifiable chain of drinking and entertainment places; but each would, on occasion, use the others and all, of course, used the same streets. Group 1 was observably the main source of disorder.

The main areas of disorder were routes to the central pubs and fast-food outlets. Large numbers congregated on these streets. The general impression was of an extremely crowded town centre, operating like a vast semi open-air party for large groups of young people. Conversations were loud and heavily laden with obscenities; their subject matter was often that of 'a good fight'. The impression that people were looking for violence or excitement was strengthened by the way the various groups did their habitual circuit of pubs and streets several times during the evening, as if continually searching. Crowds often gathered and blocked the thoroughfare outside one of the busiest, noisiest pubs, a haunt of Circuit Group 1. Broken glass lay among the cobblestones where bottles and glasses had been discarded or carelessly dropped. Mock fights, passionate embraces and verbal exercises of obscenity did not provoke the police patrols to disperse the crowds. The police were baited and jeered at.

By the Sunday of the first weekend's observations it had become clear that a noisy and violent street-culture took over the streets of central Gravesend at the weekend. No very specific scenes of violence which involved the police were observed; but violence was very close to the surface in the behaviour of these crowds of young people.

Much of the first weekend's observations had been spent within pubs and identifying the 'circuit groups' described above. Observations on the second weekend (26-28 August) changed in emphasis. Since most disorderly behaviour took place outside pubs, the observers concentrated on outside 'beats' within the main entertainment area, with only relatively quick visits to pubs to gauge the atmosphere and movement within them. As a result of this strategy more actual incidents of violence were observed. One major incident started about 10.40 pm on the Friday evening. There were already large crowds of youngsters in the vicinity of McDonalds and Windmill Street and spilling out of nearby pubs. Glass was being kicked about. Mock fights and jeering were going on. A fight looked about to start over a drunken youth who was pushed into a doorway. Two beat officers on foot ran up Windmill Street to intervene. The Police Support Unit vehicle, which had been at the top of the High Street, switched on both lights and siren and careered up Windmill Street. The crowd grew larger, joined by a large group spilling out from the take-away and more youths crowding up Windmill Street. The youths who had pushed the drunk into a doorway backed off and the two beat officers from the PSU got out and intervened in the action. The PSU must have put out a call since two more police cars entered the scene from the north end of Windmill Street. The drunken youth was bundled off at speed in a police car, lights flashing, up Windmill Street towards the police station. The crowd were very vocal and scornful of the fact that it had taken so many police officers to intervene in what they considered a minor incident. The police supervision car arrived and the duty inspector went inside the nearby pub to speak to the landlord.

By 11 pm (20 minutes after the start of the incident) one of the two beat officers had proceeded on his way and there was only one patrol car left on the scene. Two youths started shouting and pointing and began walking towards the patrol car. One of the officers had not got back into it. He and the foremost of the two youths confronted each other, one foot apart; the belligerent youth shouting and complaining at the police officer, complaining at what he saw as police over-reaction. The police officer told him to shut up or "he'd get nicked". The crowd was in sympathy with the youth and moved in closer to him. Small sub-groups of the crowd were acting out mock fights. Many girls ran up to observe the scene and were laughing and cheering the boys on. In the end the confronting youth knocked the policeman on the shoulder. At the same time it became clear that the second policeman, still in the car, had radioed for the van again. The van, containing six personnel, arrived and two foot officers. A supervision car arrived just in time to see the policeman and confronting youth now brawling on the floor. (The brawl began when the police officer informed the youth that he was arresting him for assault, after the push on the shoulder.) During the scuffle while the police officer tried to put handcuffs on the youth, his friend joined in. There were now four policemen on top of the youths on the pavement trying to arrest them. The other policemen stood between the action and the rest of the crowd trying to 'talk down' the situation. A traffic car arrived. There were now three vehicles on the scene all of which had screamed up with lights flashing and brought more crowds in their wake. The Inspector was now on the scene. It was now past closing time and staff from the nearest major pub came out from the bar to clear up glasses. The two youths were finally bundled into the van. The crowds and police began to disperse. By 11.20 pm there were only something like 60 to 70 people left on the scene and two beat officers. The excitement level had subsided. The crowd gradually dispersed on foot or to the taxi rank or McDonalds. It was nearing the end of a summer weekend evening in Gravesend. On the scene of the excitement, flower tubs were in disarray, soil had been pulled out, broken glass and a large quantity of litter was on the floor. Later on that same evening, a window was smashed in the precinct.

The above is the most dramatic incident observed in the fieldwork in Gravesend, so has been given in some detail. But observers stress that most nights the impression is given, partly aided by the relatively traffic-free nature of the town centre after 10.30 pm, of Gravesend town centre as one huge disorderly open-air pub. It was not unusual to see groups of youths carrying glasses with drink in them from pub to pub. After 10.30 pm it was common to see youths carrying bottles in their pockets or in their hands whilst wandering the streets. After the cinema had finished at 10.30 pm the town centre belonged to the 16-28 age group.

Summary of data on Cowplain and Gravesham

Ironically, the 'control' site of this pair, the area of Gravesham, and in particular its centre Gravesend, was found by our observers to present more violence and disorder than any of the six sites covered in the study. Cowplain by contrast, which has shown many violent incidents previously, appeared nothing like so disordered on the two weekends of the study.

Of course, no absolute conclusions can be drawn from a mere two weekends of observation. The levels of disorder on a given site can change amazingly quickly; sometimes as a result of police tactics (and special efforts had been made in Cowplain), sometimes as a result of shifts in population, transport arrangements or fashion. The *type* of disorder observed in Cowplain was more diffuse, more territorial, more related to rivalries between groups from different areas. Of its nature this type of disorder will be less visible to the observer than the public bacchanal of Gravesend on a summer weekend. However the observations of the fieldworkers match the findings of the message-pad analysis (see page 30 above) that in summer 1988 Gravesend presented more problems than Cowplain.

Summary and Conclusion

This chapter has concentrated on simply describing and documenting the kinds of public disorder problems discovered in our three paired sites of intensive study. The results were unexpected. We had expected the 'trouble-site' areas to show clear problems and the 'control' areas to show far less problems, and hence help to identify factors which could lead to or discourage trouble.

In the event only Haverhill and Sudbury of our paired sites showed the expected relationship. Haverhill showed continuing habitual closing time disorder; the problem in Sudbury was far less acute. Of the Woking-Guildford pair, Woking had clearly changed quite a lot since 1987. Special police efforts had been made, some troublesome entertainment venues had closed and 1988 was calmer than 1987. None the less, Woking still presented some problems. It was interesting, however, that these were not markedly more acute than those found in Guildford, which had not reported trouble in 1987. The 1988 data on both towns gives a picture of a level of disorder which seems to be almost 'normal' in entertainment centre towns. It is troublesome; but there is no feeling it is out of control. The Cowplain-Gravesham pair was different again. These were selected as examples of the cluster of rambling mixed town and country areas which had shown violence and disorder in 1987. Though the areas were demographically similar, they differed sharply in that Cowplain is on the outskirts of a large town (Portsmouth) and has no single natural centre. The area of Gravesham centres very clearly on the town of Gravesend. This difference was shown to have a very marked effect on the nature of disorder in the two areas. Gravesend itself proved to be the most troubled area we studied, although it had originally been included as a 'control' site.

What do these results tell us of the extent and nature of non-metropolitan violence in England and Wales 1988? It must be remembered that the study is not a *repeat* of the ACPO report of 1987. It is not intended as a total survey of the extent of disorder in non-metropolitan England and Wales. The ACPO report had already established that the phenomenon existed and was widespread. The function of this report is to understand it better. To the extent that some disorder was found in all the sites intensively studied, including the 'control' sites not mentioned in the ACPO report, it validates the conclusion of that report that there is a real problem

36

of non-metropolitan disorder with which we have to learn to deal. As to what this study tells us of the nature of non-metropolitan violence as observed in England and Wales in 1988, there is more still to report. The data so far from our case study sites show that the nature of disorder can vary very sharply from area to area. In the following chapter (Chapter 4) some material from surveys and group discussions relevant to the question of who exactly participates in violence will be described; Chapter 5 will bring together material from several sources on patterns of drinking and licensing; Chapter 6 will discuss the difficult role of the police. Finally Chapter 7 of this report will return to the general question of what has been learned of the nature of disorder outside the cities and how we might deal with it.

4 Drinking, disorder and the nature of participants

The ACPO report of 1987 had shown that 90% of the incidents there described involved alcohol; data presented at Chapter 3 has further demonstrated the importance of alcohol in disorder offences. To examine the connection between alcohol and disorder more closely it is necessary to look at the patterns of drinking and disorder in troubled areas: how closely (if at all) is drinking related to participation in disorder; how does the drinking of those involved in disorder compare with that of other young men; what were the social descriptors (age, class, employment status) of those who drank heavily and/or were involved in disorder?

Such questions clearly could not be answered simply by observational data. They need survey material. Ideally surveys of drinking patterns and participation in disorder would have been carried out in all six areas of intensive study. But surveys are expensive. It was decided to carry out a specimen survey in one pair of sites only; Woking and Guildford.

There is a considerable literature on methods of measuring alcohol consumption (see, for instance, Goddard and Ikin, 1988, *Drinking in England and Wales, 1987*). The methodology of the current study was worked out in the light of this existing literature. Full details and results will be given in a forthcoming publication.[1] For the moment, this chapter will concentrate on a brief presentation of those results relevant to the focus of this study.

Method of the survey

A few words must first be said as to method. It was known that young males who drink in particular trouble sites are not necessarily resident in that place. Haverhill, for instance, draws on a large rural hinterland. So do Guildford and Woking. A sample of young male drinkers in a particular location could not satisfactorily be drawn simply from residents in that location. It was hence decided to interview a sample of young males aged 16-24 who drank in either Guildford or Woking, by contacting interviewees on the street. Fieldwork was carried out between 12 and 29 August 1988 and interviews were achieved with 980 young men aged 16-24 in Guildford and 821 in Woking. Interviews were held at various sampling points throughout the Guildford and Woking areas. Each sample included both residents of the area and 'outsiders'. Local respondents formed 70% of the Guildford sample and 82% of the Woking sample. The number of 'local' respondents comprise 7%

---

[1] The survey was carried out by a commercial research firm, Research Surveys of Great Britain, under the direction of Lizanne Dowds of the Home Office Research and Planning Unit and Philip Mercieca of RSGB. It proved particularly interesting in documenting patterns of young male alcohol consumption and it is intended to publish full details as soon as feasible. Only certain central results are pulled out in the following discussion.

of the total Guildford population of 16-24 year old males and 12% of the total Woking population of 16-24 year old males. All respondents were asked certain basic questions concerning their drinking patterns; all 'heavy' drinkers and a sub-sample of 'light' drinkers were then asked follow-up questions.

Was there heavy drinking?

The surveys in both Woking and Guildford disclosed exceptionally high levels of drinking by the young male populations studied, compared to national averages previously recorded, both for England and Wales as a whole, and for non-metropolitan areas in England and Wales.

The national averages used for comparison purposes are unpublished figures from the OPCS 1987 Drinking Survey (Goddard and Ikin, 1988). The Home Office was grateful for early access to its results for the purposes of this study. Differences in methodology between the OPCS and the one reported here might well lead to some differences in reported consumption levels of the young. OPCS respondents were interviewed in the family home; respondents to the present survey in the street, often in the presence of their mates. This could be expected to lead to under-claiming of consumption by OPCS respondents, boasting over-claims by respondents to the present survey. Again, the present study, using a sample of youths actually in the street, was probably biased more to picking up the kind of sociable young men likely to be a heavy drinker; the OPCS survey conducted in the home (even though with frequent call-backs) was probably less successful at picking up heavy drinking young men.

However, even making allowances for these likely differences in response, the reported levels of drinking are surprisingly higher in Guildford and Woking than national levels. (Tables are presented at Appendix E.)

Comparisons with national average drinking patterns were (for technical reasons) made with the drinking patterns of the resident population in Guildford and Woking (omitting the 'outsiders' surveyed). However, other data within the survey showed that the drinking patterns of residents and outsiders interviewed did not greatly differ.[1]

10% of the Guildford sample and 9% of the Woking sample claimed to drink over 17+ units ($8\frac{1}{2}$ pints) on Saturday evenings (national average 7%). A similar 10% in Guildford and 7% in Woking claimed to drink 13-16 units (between $6\frac{1}{2}$ and 8 pints) on Friday evenings (national average 4%). About a third of both the Guildford and Woking sample said they drank more than 4 pints on a Friday evening; the national rate is 18%. There is a similar picture on Saturday nights, with about a third of young men in Guildford and Woking drinking more than 4 pints on a Saturday evening and one in ten (10%) drinking more than 8 pints.

---

[1] The average drinking levels of 'local residents' or 'outsiders' who were out drinking in the two towns at the weekends did not differ greatly, eg between $9\frac{1}{2}$ and $10\frac{1}{2}$ units in Guildford on Saturday nights. Note these are *average* drinking rates for young men aged 16-24 who go out drinking. About five pints a night on at least one of the two main weekend evenings is the 'normal' consumption in these two towns for those of this age group who do go out drinking on Friday or Saturday nights.

The national figures are 21% drinking more than 4 pints on Saturday evenings and 7% drinking more than 8 pints.

Not all young men in Guildford and Woking are drinking so much. It is worth noting that something over a third of the sample drank nothing on Friday evening and a similar proportion did not drink on Saturday evening.

The great majority of drinking took place in pubs on both Friday and Saturday nights in both towns, although Friday is the heaviest pub-going night (76% of drinkers in Guildford had been to a pub on Friday night, 72% in Woking). Saturday night pub-using figures fell to 62% and 59% respectively. Heavy drinkers tended to use pubs more than light drinkers.

All the above data has been presented for 16-24 year olds, although 16-17 year olds are, of course, below the legal age for public-house drinking. Table 9, Appendix E, compares the drinking of this sample of 16-17 year olds with 18-24 year olds. On their heaviest drinking night, the average amount drunk by 16-17 year olds in these two towns ($2\frac{1}{2}$ to $3\frac{1}{2}$ pints) was rather less than the average of older drinkers; but was still more than OPCS national estimates would have predicted. Of all the 16-17 year olds contacted by this study, 30% (almost one third) claimed to have been out drinking in pubs on at least one night the previous weekend – although this is, of course, for them, an illegal habit.

How much disorder was seen?

The survey has disclosed a pattern of heavy drinking by the young in Guildford and Woking. Did these young men witness much disorder?

About half the young men interviewed in each town had seen at least one incident of disorder in the twelve months leading up to the interview. Just over a third had witnessed between 1 and 10 incidents and 14% in Guildford and 8% in Woking had witnessed 11 or more disturbances. Of all the incidents witnessed by the total sample, over 80% were said to be related to drinking, something over 5% not related, and the respondents were unsure concerning the remainder. It seems beyond doubt that most disorder is related to drinking patterns.

Some of the witnessed incidents appeared fairly serious (those who had witnessed incidents were asked to list details about the three most recent incidents they had seen). While about 42% of these incidents involved five or less people, 37% involved 6 to 20 people and about 9% involved more than 20 people. Some respondents may of course have witnessed and been remembering the same incidents as others. Apart from the number of people involved there are other indicators as to the seriousness of the incident. Respondents were asked whether anyone was hurt or any property damaged in the incident where the greatest number of people was involved. It was reported that someone was hurt in about half of these incidents and that property was damaged in 19% of the incidents in Guildford and 26% in Woking. The data suggest that it is not uncommon in these two towns for youngsters to have witnessed a number of fights or disturbances and that some of these incidents may have been fairly serious.

Respondents were also asked if the incidents that they witnessed involved mainly locals, mainly outsiders or both. In Guildford, 36% of incidents witnessed were claimed to involve outsiders (either mainly outsiders or both outsiders and locals) compared with 28% in Woking. It is interesting that when asked who were the outsiders involved, 75% of respondents in Guildford and 44% in Woking named 'soldiers' or 'squaddies', as the outsiders involved. This leads on to the next question that the survey was intended to help answer.

Who was involved in disorder?

Ever since the publicity given to the ACPO report findings, there has been much public discussion as to who exactly were the participants. Were they 'yuppie yobboes', 'hooray henries', 'lager louts' or the poor and the deprived?

The socio-economic and other data on the nature of admitted participants in violence can tell us a little more about the kind of young men they were. Of all the young men interviewed, 13% said that they had been involved in an incident or disorder. Looking more closely at these 207 cases, they tend to be mostly 18-24 year olds, employed, and semi-skilled or unskilled manual workers. However, this is not particularly revealing as the same is also true for the group who had not been involved in any disorder. Looking at the *differences* between the 'participants' and 'non-participants' there is evidence of an emerging pattern as to what is important in predicting who will become involved in disorder. In relation to the demographic data, 72% of participators had left school at 16 or 17 while only 49% of the non-participators had left school by this age. In terms of actual ages, although most participators were aged 18-24, 33% of participators were aged 16 or 17 compared with 23% of non-participants. Looking at work status, although most participators were employed, 19% of them were unemployed compared with 8% of non-participators, and 18% of participators were still in full-time education compared with 28% of non-participators. Excluding those still in full-time education and looking just at the economically active, 22% of participants came from managerial and professional classes as against 31% of non-participators. Finally (and not perhaps surprisingly) of those involved in disorder, 64% were 'heavy' drinkers. (Heavy drinkers are defined as those who drank more than 8 units on at least one weekend evening.)

These data suggest that young men who drink heavily, who left school at 16 or 17, who are unemployed and who are semi-skilled or unskilled manual workers are more likely to become involved in disorder. Some of these variables may be more important than others; the imbalance between participators and non-participators in terms of heavy and light drinking is the most striking one while the social class difference is the least marked. The next section explores the nature of the participators in more depth.

The group discussions

The description of the difference between participants and non-participants in disorder and violence given above was based on survey data. It was further validated and enriched through some 'group discussions' held in Guildford and

Woking in the week following the survey. Respondents who claimed in the survey to have participated in or witnessed violent incidents, were asked if they would be willing to attend such discussions. Four group discussions were conducted, two in Guildford and two in Woking, with interviewees drawn from this source. In each town one group discussion was with claimed 'participants', the other with claimed 'onlookers'.

The group discussions were held in rooms in central pubs in each town and were conducted by an experienced moderator (Mr Bob Lucas), provided by the market research company Questel Ltd. The turn-out for each group was good and the discussion lively but friendly. Respondents were offered a drink in order to induce a relaxed atmosphere. The only topics on which respondents were reticent were those of their own criminal records and the extent to which they had themselves instigated violence; otherwise there was nothing upon which they were not prepared to give an opinion.

The moderator was particularly struck by the overt difference between the groups of 'participants' and 'onlookers' and since his comments seem to be both perceptive, and to reflect the differences between the two groups which emerged from the survey data, it seems worthwhile quoting his comments in full:—

"This study was relatively small therefore it might be unwise to draw firm conclusions on the differences between participants and onlookers. None the less these differences were so marked that it is considered useful to include some observations that might shed light on further findings.

Participants were noticeably more overtly macho then onlookers. They were more likely to be scruffily dressed – T-shirts and jeans – and to be adorned with symbols of male toughness – tattoos and big boots. While they were vociferous and forthcoming they were mostly not very articulate and found it impossible to talk without swearing; swearing being a verbal equivalent of a tattoo – ie, a reinforcement of masculinity. That aside they were a very pleasant and friendly to each other and the moderator.

Almost all of them had jobs but these were usually of a very basic kind – postman, caretaker, labourer, forecourt attendant – with little or no career prospects. Jobs were felt to be easy to find as long as one was not choosy.

One or two had opted for unemployment on the argument that it was better to be unemployed than to have a poorly paid job with no future.

There was a predominant feeling amongst the participants that society had very little to offer them except a boring job or on the dole. There was also considerable resentment that their school qualifications meant very little. One respondent claimed that he had eight CSEs but still could not find a job with a future in which he could take pride. Another complained of having to fill in a long application form and go through a battery of psychological tests in order to become a sweeper in a post office, yet another describes his difficulty in obtaining a small grant (£120) for a course that would have taught him a useful skill.

Participants typically exhibited a short term view of life. When it came to talking about any fulfilments the common theme was instant gratification – women, fast cars, holidays and being rich in order to obtain these. The people they admired or envied were people who in their view had achieved these goals – Prince Charles (attractive wife, lots of money), Don Johnson (star of Miami Vice, cars, pretty girls, expensive clothes, money), Rod Stewart and Peter Stringfellow (for the same reasons). When they talked about what they would do with a large amount of money (e.g. £100,000) the themes were the same and usually involved spending it on instant fun with no thought for the future.

Hope or lack of it, appeared to play quite a strong part in determining such attitudes. The main difference between participants and onlookers seemed to be in the degree to which they had accepted or not that they had a role to play in society; participants could not see a career ahead of them, their qualifications (such as they were) were useless to them, they had not yet taken on responsibilities of their own (a house, marriage, children). They often appeared to believe that society had let them down and to resent this.

It should be emphasised here that respondents did not seek to explain or excuse their participation in violent incidents by the arguments that society was to blame. Discussion of prospects and the nature of society was entirely separate from that of violence. None the less, it seems probable that if a young man feels rejected by society, a failure in an increasingly achievement-orientated society, he would be less likely to wish to restrict his behaviour in order to abide by the rules of that society.

There were exceptions to the typical participant outlined above. Disconcertingly one or two of them had good jobs (e.g. electrician) and were clearly not 'hopeless' in their outlook on life. It is impossible to say whether or not this pattern is reflected in society as a whole on the basis of this study.

Onlookers differed strongly from participants. One cannot help but feel that this may simply be a quirk of the sample, after all we only spoke to two groups of each type. However, it is felt that these differences may be instructive and they are therefore listed below.

The onlookers were smarter in their appearance than the participants and clearly took more care over the impression they gave through their appearance to other people. Some came to the discussion in office clothes, others were smartly casual. They were also more articulate than the participants and more circumspect in the opinions they gave, that is to say they took pains to avoid offending other respondents and to be reasonable when stating a case. They came from a wide variety of backgrounds (ex public school through to council estates) and represented a good range of occupations (estate agents, electricians, students, labourers).

Their outlook on life was definitely more optimistic than that of the participants. They felt privileged to live in the prosperous South (especially Guildford), they felt that the country was generally on the right road and that they would be able to improve their lot over time. This was not so much a political attitude as a general belief that there were jobs and opportunity aplenty in their area. They acknowledged that they might well have had a different opinion had they come from the North.

At the same time, the way they described violent incidents differed little from the participants. They had all experienced identical situations with the obvious exception that the degree of involvement was different.

Thus, on the basis of necessarily limited observation, one is tempted to the conclusion that we are faced with two clear types of people.

Participants who are disillusioned because they feel they can play no useful role in society, poorly educated and with either dead-end jobs or no job (of their own choice), who seek to define themselves by exaggerated male behaviour – both symbolic (tattoos and swearing) and physical.

Onlookers who may have similar backgrounds to Participants but who might generally be expected to have derived more from education, have jobs that satisfy their needs, have better prospects and therefore have greater self-esteem and a sense of belonging in society and less desire to assert themselves through violence."

A major subject matter of discussion in all groups was the nature and possible causes of violence. Not surprisingly, these young men from their own particular isolated perspectives, were no more able to provide total answers to these problems than were the many pundits who have considered such issues since the publication of the ACPO report findings. None the less, their insights are interesting and at least have the value of being based on experience. Their views were summarised by the group discussant as follows:—

"All respondents had either been involved in or had witnessed violence associated with excess alcohol. Their experiences had all been broadly similar whether they had been participants or onlookers. Very few had experienced the same incident which made it difficult to discuss specific events.

In both Woking and Guildford violence on Fridays and Saturdays was said to be endemic and inevitable. Violence in Guildford was described as being as bad as it possibly could be with people using baseball bats, knives and other weapons, however Woking was acknowledged to be the more violent of the two.

Single straightforward motivations for violence were impossible to isolate. It has a long history in both towns but especially Woking. No important reasons for violence emerged; possibilities such as race, unemployment and gang rivalry were discussed but rejected in all discussions. Race was not said to be a problem, quite a few participants had Black or Asian friends. Unemployment is not a real problem, although career jobs could be difficult to find. Gangs or identifiable groups of young men were said to have died out in both towns, though they had once existed.

Respondents were of the opinion that violence was normal – 'these are violent times' and most could identify no real root cause behind it. Some people blamed a general moral corruption, the breakdown of established religion, the lack of parental authority, violence on the part of the police, but they were a minority and found little support from other members of the groups. Needless to say it is impossible to comment on such cosmic issues on the basis of the study.

Thus, depressingly, we are left with a picture of a generation for whom violence is a part of life with no apparent motive behind it, inevitable and showing no sign of going away. We have seen that certain features of Woking contribute to violent incidents but these features are not present in Guildford therefore one is wary of putting them forward as *causes* of violence. Thus the conclusion is that the threshold of violence has risen in these towns for reasons that are obscure or too deeply entrenched to be uncovered in a study of this type.''

The above quotation shows that though the group discussions were illuminating on differences between participants and non-participants in violence, they did not take matters much further on the *causes* of violence, unless to show that the causes were opaque to the young men themselves. There certainly seemed to be no obvious political, racial or gang motivation. Before leaving the account of the group discussions it may be worth quoting the discussant's summary of how the youths themselves described 'typical' incidents:—

''Friday and Saturday nights were felt to be the main danger points for violence. Friday especially was considered as a likely night for violence because this was the night when groups of young men would get together and inevitably have too much to drink. Drinking alcohol was inextricably linked with a good social life.

The most likely time for trouble would be after the pubs had shut when these groups of young men would be on the streets, usually drunk but still wanting something to do and coming up against similar groups.

The same essential sequence of events was related by everybody. Violence could be triggered by seemingly trivial events. It could be brushing past someone or even just *looking* at someone. An argument would develop – 'what the f_____ are you looking at?' – and escalate verbally to the stage of mild physical involvement – pushing and shoving – and from there it would be but one step to a fight. When groups were involved the 'code' would necessitate members supporting each other:

''Groups can take anyone on.''

The key to this pattern is 'machismo', reinforced in this case by the group. If you are the person who is stared at or brushed past you have to make an issue of it, the more so if you had some of your drink spilt. You cannot let it go in front of your friends. Equally, if you are the offender you cannot let any challenge go unanswered, you have to stand up for yourself or lose face.

There was said to be very little organised violence; that is to say events in which people go out for the sole reason of having a fight. There had been occasions in the past, it was said, when youths from Surbiton and even Wimbledon travelled to Woking by train for a fight but this was said to have died out. There were also tales of inter-council estate fights that had some degree of planning but none of our respondents had had direct experience of these.

Finally, nobody claimed to be the instigator of violent action, it was always imposed on them by other forces and they had no choice but to respond. This suggests that participants find it easy to justify their action as self-defence. There was no doubt however that a certain amount of 'glory' was involved, people often recounted with relish skirmishes in which they had taken part.

From the onlookers point of view it could seem less glorious. They described incidents in which they had been attacked because they came from the wrong area or had a silly hat on or equally senseless reasons.

One is left with the feeling that fights occur on very little pretext and that while they may be unplanned, they are as unavoidable as if they had been planned. This seems to suggest that the real problem in those towns is the innate aggression of the young male rather than any identifiable and changeable cause.''

Under-age drinking and disorder

One point that should perhaps be discussed briefly in this section is the specific issue of under-age drinking and violence. The survey results showed that 16 and 17 year olds in Woking and Guildford appeared to be drinking heavily in comparison with their national counterparts (although not in comparison with 18-24 year olds in Woking and Guildford) and that nearly a third of under-age young men had a drink in a pub in Guildford or Woking the previous weekend. It also appears that 16-17 year olds are disproportionately more likely to become involved in disorder. It may be that 16-17 year olds will always become involved in disorder regardless of whether they drink at all or how much they drink. However, if the sample is divided into heavy and light drinkers, 35% of heavy-drinking 16-17 year olds became involved in disorder compared with 12% of light or non-drinkers. If the amount they drank was of no importance, one would expect the same proportion to get into trouble. But it should be remembered in interpreting these results that 'light' drinkers will include those who do not go out to pubs at all and therefore have no 'opportunity' to become involved in disorder. It is possible that reducing under-age drinking could be relevant to the control of disorder and this point will be discussed further in the final chapter. However, it must be remembered that the majority of those involved in disorder were 18-24 year olds (page 4).

Summary and conclusion

This chapter has presented data from the survey of drinking and disorder carried out in Guildford and Woking in summer 1988 and from the ensuing group discussions held in both areas. Young people were found to drink very heavily especially on Fridays and Saturdays. Their consumption in alcoholic units was higher than that suggested in national bench-mark studies, although this may be due to the use of a different methodology. (The present study would be likely to pick up more active and sociable young men.)

A picture of the characteristic heavy drinker and participant in weekend disorder was built up. He was characteristically young, employed in a low-status job, went drinking in male groups and seemed to be inspired by a search for entertainment or weekend distraction rather than by any more serious motivation. There was a considerable amount of under-age drinking and 16-17 year olds are disproportionately likely to become involved in disorder.

5 Patterns and places of drinking: lessons for prevention

This chapter will explore some implications of typical patterns of drinking and disorder for the possible prevention of such disorder. It will draw on observational, analytic and survey material.

The young men in the groups had been quite clear that "the most likely time for trouble would be after the pubs had shut ... when they were on the streets ... still wanting something to do" (page 45). This was also the experience of the observational fieldworkers; and the same pattern is shown in police message-pad data. Figure 1, page 48 shows the peaking of calls to the police concerning public disorder incidents at closing time – a result which has been paralleled in earlier studies of entertainment centre violence (Hope 1985, Ramsay 1982).

It is worth exploring a little further, drawing in particular on fieldwork observations in the six areas studied, the way evening patterns of drink and disorder typically develop. There is an interaction between pubs, clubs and late-night take-aways, the number and placing of all these affecting the way the evening's entertainment develops.

Disorder usually occurs at or around some sort of 'entertainment centre' whether they are whole town centres (such as Haverhill, Guildford, Woking, Gravesend) or more scattered sub-centres (eg Waterlooville Centre in Cowplain). Most areas contain a range of different pubs and clubs, entertainment venues and fast-food outlets. Guildford, an example of an entertainment centre, has a Civic Hall on the north-east outskirts of the town which has occasional pop-concerts and facilities for private discos; at least seven popular pubs in the town centre, plus a bar below a restaurant; two night-clubs (both in the centre of the town, both open until 2 am) and five popular fast-food outlets near the centre of the town (a Kebab House, a Kentucky Fried Chicken, a McDonalds, a Pizza Hut and a Wimpy). Haverhill, a smaller town than Guildford, still has a range of entertainment outlets. There are a number of small public houses in the main street; a Football Club (which at the time of the study had regular Friday night discos), a night-club which was licensed only for normal pub hours but had a disco every night of the week, a late-night pool club, away from the centre; and fast-food take-away outlets in the High Street. All areas showed a similar mix of places to go.

Across the six case-study areas, similar patterns of drinking were observed among the young men most likely to be the main source of disorder. The following is a composite picture – but generally true of all areas observed. Friday and Saturday nights were the main drinking nights with Friday most likely to be the heavy drinking night with the lads, although the same pattern could occur on Saturdays. Typically the young men would go out with a group of three to five others. They

Figure 1

Rate of occurrence of public disorder incidents by hour over the weekend

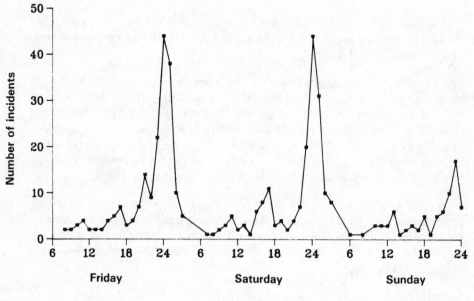

NOTES:

Source: message pads.

Number of incidents = 443.

The plot covers the period 0601 Friday morning to 2400 Sunday night. Each point on the plot represents one hour of this period. The vertical axis shows the total number of public disorder incidents recorded during that hour over 9 weekends and 6 areas.

The total number of public disorder incidents for each hour is therefore based on incidents accumulated during 54 'occasions', where an occasion equals a particular weekend in a particular area.

Hence to obtain the average incident rate, over all occasions, for a given hour of the weekend, the total number for that hour shown on the plot above should be divided by the 54 occasions on which it occurred. For example, for the hour Friday 2301-2400 there is a total of 44 incidents shown. Divided by 54, this yields a rate of 0.8 incidents per hour on the average occasion.

The peak hours for offending, as plotted above, are 2301-2400 Friday and Saturday, and 2201-2300 Sunday.

like to go to the loud, bouncy, heavy drinking pubs which they favour, when these are already beginning to be lively and crowded. This means that the evening's serious drinking often starts nearer 9 pm than 6 pm or 7 pm, although some groups will have met earlier at quieter pubs. The favourite pubs for Friday night serious drinking will be very crowded and may well have disco music; although no space for dancing. Drinking is rapid and in rounds. Between 9 and 11 pm many lads will have taken in over eight pints. There is not a lot of conversation and what there is is loud and raucous over the accompanying loud music. The pubs are probably very crowded. 11 pm is closing time. At many pubs bar staff are anxious to clear up and go home. Within about ten minutes, youths now well tanked-up and excited are ejected on to the street, sometimes carrying their take-away cans of more beer. Some – but not the young and excitable – may then go home. If they're lucky they may go to the home of one of their mates to continue the evening's drinking. But many cannot go back to the parental home – or just don't want to. For them the evening is just beginning. They wander down to the local fast-food take-aways then stand about watching the talent, talking, waiting and hoping to meet someone or for something to happen. Many of our observers thought this 'watching' part of the evening – outside the take-aways – was the serious part of the evening to which the rest was preliminary. Inevitably, some of the lads (many of whom are very young) are over-excited or have drunk too much. Then an incident happens. Drunks stumble against each other, or insults are passed. Perhaps the proprietor of the local take-away feels he has to call the police. Then siren-cars draw up screaming – or perhaps some foot-patrol officers appear quietly. Whatever it is, the appearance of the police becomes part of the entertainment. There is something to watch. The crowds get more excited, jeer and taunt the police. Perhaps the whole incident calms down and the lads disappear homeward. Perhaps it escalates – and there is another incident of public disorder of the sort recorded in the ACPO report. The ACPO report documented about five such incidents per week in the whole of non-metropolitan England and Wales. Not a great many perhaps. But the case studies recorded in this report suggests the *potential* for such incidents is regularly there every Friday or Saturday in many – if not most – of the many entertainment centres, some large, some small, in non-metropolitan England and Wales.

It is a pattern of entertainment drinking which seems to be peculiar to the United Kingdom. Similar drinking patterns have already been well-documented in UK metropolitan entertainment centres (Ramsay, 1982; Ashley, 1984; Hope, 1985; describing Southampton, Sunderland and Newcastle). In Europe there is no regular closing time; so one does not get the united sudden exodus on to the streets. In the United States, some similar patterns of street-bacchanal – almost street parties – are found in reasonably upper-class entertainment areas such as Georgetown bars and take-aways in Washington, where the streets on summer nights are full of young people wandering between them; or the Westwood Campus of the University of California in Los Angeles. But routinely American bars are quieter, less raucous places than British pubs; social drinking is done at private parties; in most places the streets are simply not safe enough to turn into places of public entertainment for the very young. The UK pattern is a traditional one. It occurs in towns and cities as well as non-metropolitan areas. It does not always cause trouble. The rest of this chapter will discuss factors which seem to cause this traditional UK pattern of drinking, either to erupt into violence or remain manageable. Only factors concerned with the locations and patterns of drinking and of management of licensed and fast-food outlets will be considered. The role of the police will be considered in Chapter 6.

The nature of licences: 'youth pubs' and entertainment licences

It has sometimes been suggested that increasing problems of non-metropolitan disorder are connected with a proliferation of late-night entertainment licences. Licensing statistics for the six case-study areas were examined to see if this were so (Appendix F). It will be seen that the number of club licences had not increased between 1982 and 1986 in either the 'trouble-site' areas or the controls. There had however been an increase in the number of licensed public houses in the two 'trouble-site' areas of Havant (including Cowplain) and Woking; this may well be connected with the growth in the youth population of these areas in the same period (see page 29 above). The police message-pad data for the six case-study areas showed that even in towns where late-night licensing (until 2 am) did exist, the peak hour for disorder was still the hour immediately after pub closing (page 48).

The reason for this may have something to do with the nature of the clientele of late-night music and dancing clubs. Several were observed in different towns in the course of this study. Characteristically they draw the slightly better-off end of the youth market. A common pattern is for youngsters who may have already spent a couple of hours in a public house with loud disco, to go on from there (possibly via a fast-food joint) to a late-night club. At the club there is again loud music but this time usually accompanied by dancing. The peak crowded hour is usually about midnight. Customers gradually taper away before the final closing hour of 2 am. It is the impression of the observers that by the time the final customers of the late night joints fade away in the early hours of the morning, they are physically fairly exhausted, have 'wound down' and do not feel the need or have the energy for raucous street gatherings. It is those at the poorer end of the youth market who do not go on to the late-night clubs, but issue straight from the pub discos to the street, who are the tinder waiting for the spark of disorder. There can, on occasion, be dispersal problems after the 2 am closing of the clubs – some were reported from Sudbury – but these are rarely major public order incidents. It was interesting that some senior police in Haverhill (the 'trouble-site' town from which Sudbury was the control) felt that Haverhill's problems might be eased if there were a late-night licensed club in the town (there were none at the time of the fieldwork).

Some have suggested that the greater salience of youth disorder of recent years may be connected with the growth in 'youth pubs'. It is a reasonable hypothesis (and one borne out by the observations of this study) that where age-groups mix in public houses, older men have some sort of restraining influence on the young. But in recent years there has been a growth in pubs, the decor, arrangements and music of which are designed especially to appeal to the young. Characteristically such pubs will have at a minimum a good jukebox, and usually also, on Friday or

Saturday, a regular 'disco'. A pub does not require a special licence of any sort to run a disco so long as not more than two people are running it. Late-night clubs or venues with an entertainment licence for music and dancing have to meet quite stringent conditions, including fire regulations, having a specified minimum amount of dance-floor space, regulations on the numbers allowed in. None of these conditions apply to disco pubs. Such pubs, packing in youngsters wall-to-wall to listen to loud continuous sound while drinking but not dancing, seem to be far less regulated than outlets with entertainment licences for music and dancing, and to have the potential to cause much more trouble. Yet the disco pubs are very profitable. One landlord interviewed, who had converted his pub to a youth-disco venue over the last year, was already making enough profits to be thinking of selling up and buying a bar in Spain.

It is sometimes suggested that 'youth pubs' should be discouraged or their numbers controlled or minimised. Yet this is not necessarily the right solution. It is not easy, or necessarily sensible, to control natural movements of the market. Interviews with licensees, young men and police across our case-study areas, indicated that there was a growing pattern, in those areas of Southern England, for traditional country pubs to be converted into restaurants with bars; places to attract the prosperous middle-class, middle-age groups out from the population centres such as Guildford or Woking for evenings out 'in the country'; and for town centre pubs to be converted into 'youth-pubs' or 'disco-pubs' attracting in the young from the towns themselves and from surrounding villages to meet their peers and have a night out. Some Woking drinkers complained they *had* to go into Woking town centre to find other youngsters; the pubs in their home villages had been turned into up-market family restaurant pubs.

This kind of movement of the market is probably irresistible. The brewers and licensees are merely responding to natural movements in demand, probably connected with greater mobility and prosperity. But there are possibly lessons for the brewers in how 'youth-pubs' could and should be managed. It might be desirable that some special form of licence, with conditions, should be devised for the 'disco-pub'. These points will be further considered in the final chapter of this report.

The management of pubs

Even with current licensing arrangements there are steps pub managers can take to minimise disorder. It should be said immediately that, almost without exception, the pubs visited in all our case-study towns were well-managed and did not appear to generate disorder within their own walls. They were perhaps routinely careless in serving under-age drinkers (the survey data, page 46 above, shows how common such drinking is) but this is a notoriously difficult legal provision to implement, to which we shall return in Chapter 6 when possible police strategies are considered. But even though the pubs in our samples were pretty generally successful in reducing within-pub disorder, they turned out customers in varying states of excitement.

The 'good' pub takes time to eject its customers. The bar staff start clearing away glasses and empty bottles early. The music is turned down at least ten minutes before people begin to be turned out of the doors. The manager is himself visibly present. There are bouncers by the doors urging people not to hang around by the doors even when waiting for someone else. The duty to wind the customers down a bit, to take things gradually, is observed. The 'bad' pub (from the point of view of generating disorder outside) takes closing time at a rush; loud music is played to the last minute, there is no early collection of empties, youngsters are hurled outside very rapidly, still 'high', there is no attempt to encourage them to disperse. Six packs are sold rapidly even to the visibly drunk.

The location of pubs and take-aways

One factor which could usefully be considered by either brewers (when considering conversion to a youth-pub) or by planning or licensing authorities would be the actual geographic location of the pub, club or take-away.

Disorder characteristically happens in quite small central locations – around high streets or shopping centres, where pubs, clubs and take-aways are clustered. It is arguable that problems could be minimised if youth club and take-aways did not group at some particular entertainment centre but were dispersed across neighbourhoods. But both commercial reality and customer demand lead inevitably to concentration. Half the reason why young people go out is to be with each other. Again the concentration of outlets can be useful, if it means the entertainment centre is drawn away from residential areas to an area of offices and shops. Entertainment centres grow at centres of transport. A sufficiency of transport away from the entertainment centre late at night is important, if disorder is to be prevented.

Observers in this study felt that some distinction should be made between 'clustering' and 'congestion' within entertainment centres. 'Cluster points' within entertainment centres are outdoor locations where people are likely to gather and remain for a period of time. From time immemorial there have been such 'cluster points' where there are human settlements. The lads of the village would gather by the bridge across a river, or at some other central location, to stand about and chat and eye the passing girls. The citizens of a town would know on which streets to walk to meet their neighbours. 'Congestion points' are quite different. They are on thoroughfares where large groups of people are likely to be moving from one area to another and where they might collide.

Occasionally in these case studies, observers could identify 'cluster points' which were also 'congestion points'. There is an example in the Windmill Street precinct in Gravesend. This is a cluster point for people drinking at a major and popular pub and eating at nearby take-away fast-food outlets. But it is also a congestion point since passers-by going, for instance, from the Railway to the Clocktower area, need to pass through the Windmill Street area. By contrast, there were other cluster points in Gravesend which were not routinely sites of congestion.

It was not only the observational work which pointed to 'situational' effects on public disorder. The analysis of police message-pad data showed how incidents of disorder (especially those that involved drink) clustered routinely at particular locations *within* entertainment centre areas.

It could be useful if maps of location of disorder were made for all entertainment centres and could be routinely available to licensing justices, managers of take-away food chains, crime prevention officials and the general public. Location is clearly crucial to the incidence of disorder and, over the years, gradual work could be done to try to ensure that pubs, clubs and take-away outlets did not cluster at congestion points, but were disposed as to allow natural gatherings of young people without encouraging conflict. Police message-pad data could be used to make such analyses.

In many ways this is a planning issue. The town planners of the past (back as far as those, lost in the mists of time, who invented village greens) understood that settlements, be they villages, towns or cities, needed room for 'the promenade', 'the paseo', the place where citizens, especially the young, could walk, could linger, could meet. Too often the need for such spaces is forgotten in modern town planning, which is built around daytime not evening or entertainment use. Town and village planners need to recover the art of planning for natural social gatherings. Such gatherings will occur, whether the planners allow the space for it or not. But where there is congestion, or insufficient space, the chances of public disorder are maximised.

Safety and management of fast-food outlets

All these points about the siting of pubs and clubs are also applicable to the siting of fast-food outlets. Observers in this study found that most late-night fast-food outlets were (as were the pubs) well-managed. They were not in themselves sites of disorder. But much depended on their placing on the high streets or shopping precincts of the various towns. Consideration needs to be given both by the planning authorities and by the managers of fast-food chains to the siting of popular outlets. They will inevitably become late-night cluster points. They need not inevitably become congestion points.

Thought perhaps also needs to be given to the staffing of these outlets, late at night, in possible disorder areas. Some employ 'bouncers' or security staff, or make sure that senior experienced staff are on hand who can judge how to handle young people and when it is wise to call the police. Some (the minority) are left in the control of very young staff, who do not have the skills to manage potential trouble-makers of the same age as themselves.

Closing time

Before turning to the difficult question of policing for entertainment centre disorder (Chapter 6 following), a word should be said about the likely effect of the new extension of licensing hours under the Licensing Act 1988. This came into force in September 1988 just after the date of the fieldwork for this study. Under the new licensing regulations, pubs have greater freedom to set their own opening hours during the day. But closing time still remains fixed at 11 pm, even for pubs in the

town centre. It is just possible that some people may start drinking earlier on
Fridays and Saturdays because of the new regulations, and not be able to go on
drinking so long and that hence the mass ejection of drinkers on to the street at 11
pm may become less marked. But this seems unlikely, given the fact (page 49
above) that most young men appear not to wish to begin their drinking proper until
the pubs are reasonably crowded. However, it might be worth repeating the survey
for Guildford and Woking at some later date to see if the new licensing laws have
affected patterns of evening drinking.

Summary and conclusion

In this chapter the pattern of a typical weekend night out in a non-metropolitan area
has been described. There is an interaction between pubs and late-night take-aways.
It has been suggested that, although most entertainment outlets are already
reasonably well-managed, there is room for more careful planning, both by those
responsible for town or area land-usage plans and by owners of pub or take-away
outlets, to try to ensure that both the siting and management of outlets is such as
to minimise disorder.

6 Policing strategies and lessons for prevention

So far this report has analysed the location of disorder offences in England and Wales (Chapter 2); described the kind of disorder which occurs at six exemplary sites (Chapter 3); described the kind of young man who becomes involved in both heavy drinking and disorder offences (Chapter 4); and suggested some lessons to be learned about the problems of managing drinking.

The police have the difficult task of controlling and dealing with the kind of drunken disorder which this report describes. In this chapter evidence about the tasks and difficulties of the police will be presented from three sources:—

(a) From the police message-pad data gathered in the six areas studied in July and August 1988.

(b) From the survey and group discussions in Guildford and Woking in August 1988.

(c) From the observational work and interviews carried out in six weeks in August 1988.

The police message pads and dealing with disorder

It will be remembered that, as part of this study, arrangements were made to collate all incidents of disorder recorded on police message pads in the nine weekends of July and August 1988 in the six areas selected for intensive study (page 16 above). Incidents of disorder were defined as public events and taken to exclude (unless they happen on the street) domestic disputes, landlord-tenant disputes or any other where the setting was wholly private property. Disorder in places which were privately owned but open to the public (eg shops, stations, pubs) were included. Key words sought in message pads were 'trouble, rowdies, kids, youths, gang, yobs, noise, disturbance, fight, assault, dispute, conflict'.

The set of police message-pad incidents runs somewhat wider than the incident set discussed by the ACPO report. The ACPO report focused on incidents where there were large numbers of offenders and the police had difficulty in mobilising a response. The message pads include incidents from the most serious to the most trivial (such as complaints about minor scuffles or noisy motor-cyclists). A total of 447 such incidents were recorded on message pads over the six areas and nine weekends studied. Of these 447 incidents, 26% (114 incidents) were recorded as definitely drink-related (although more may have involved drink without this fact finding its way on to the message pad). The peak hours both for all incidents and all drink-related incidents were the hours between 11 pm and midnight on Friday and Saturday and to a lesser extent between 10 pm and 11 pm on Sunday (see Fig 1, page 48), ie the hour after closing time. That this is the peak hour for all disorder offences (even for those where the alcohol connection is not formally recorded) suggests that alcohol in general and pub drinking in particular have a role to play in most public disorder. This is not surprising. Pub hours control the times of public gatherings and it is when groups are gathered together that disorder is most likely to occur.

The rate of incidents reported at the peak hour in individual areas ranged from 0 to 5 but only about 1 in 16 occasions involved 3 or more and the average across all 6 towns and all weekends was just 0.8/hour.

The great majority of incidents (70%) recorded on message pads were dealt with by one police unit alone, although whether this was by choice or necessity was not directly known; nor was it possible to obtain reliable information on the size of the police units dispatched. Second wave reinforcements were rare. However, more units were sent to incidents mentioning violence. Over a third of pub, food and community premises incidents received two or more units.

Twenty-nine per cent of incident records ended with the terse abbreviations "GOA" (gone on arrival) or "ASNT"(area searched no trace) . Twenty-three per cent were recorded as "all quiet, advice given". One in eight incidents resulted in arrest and caution or charging – an average of just over 2 people arrested for every incident with an arrest. Violence-related incidents were more likely to end in arrest; eighteen per cent of them did so.

If one takes these statistics of police response at face-value, the impression is given that disorder put relatively limited strain on police resources. Second-wave reinforcements are rarely seen on message pads and the frequency of incidents resulting in arrests is low. However, incidents peak markedly at closing time. Does this generally bland picture conceal sudden intensive demand which can overstrain resources? In an attempt to explore this question further, the relationship between police disorder workload and police response in numbers of units was plotted for all hours, over the nine weekends studied, in the six intensive case-study areas. Hours over the whole weekend were plotted in ascending order of demand, (ie, of numbers of disorder calls in a given hour. This is the horizontal axis of Figure 2 p.57). The number of police units dispatched to incidents of disorder in the same hours were then plotted against these, in the same ordering of hours (this is the vertical axis of Figure 3). In an ideal world, the resulting plot should be a straight diagonal; the number of police units dispatched would rise in proportion to the numbers of incidents occurring. As Figure 2 shows, this is broadly true; but there is a marked flattening of the diagonal at the hours where between 20 and 40 incidents an hour (for all case-study areas over all weekends) are being recorded on police message-pads. This is prima facie evidence that at these times the police are having difficulty in responding to calls for help at the normal rate. Further inspection of the data showed that these hours, where difficulty appeared to be experienced in responding in proportion to demand, were the hours between 12 midnight and 1 am on Friday and Saturday, ie the hours *after* two of the principal peaks of the weekend (the peak hours themselves are on the diagonal). It is possible

Figure 2

Number of patrol units dispatched against number of incidents recorded each hour

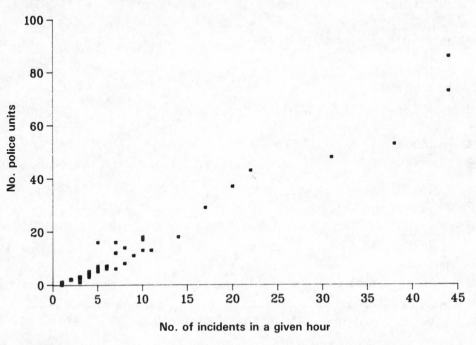

NOTES:

Source: message pads.

Number of incidents = 443.

The plot covers the period 0601 Friday morning to 2400 Sunday night. Each point on the plot represents one hour of this period, and has two scores. The horizontal axis shows the total number of public disorder incidents recorded over 9 weekends and 6 areas, for the hour in question; the vertical axis shows, for the same hours, the total number of patrol units dispatched in response to these incidents.

The patrol unit score for each hour is therefore based on information from incidents accumulated during 54 'occasions', where an occasion equals a particular weekend in a particular area. Hence to obtain the average over all occasions for a given hour of the weekend, the total number of patrol units dispatched for that hour, plotted above, should be divided by the 54 occasions on which it was based.

The incident score for each hour is accumulated in the same way, and the process is described in more detail on Figure 1.

The hours on this plot are not arranged in chronological order, but ranked according to their scores on each axis. The hour whose point is at the extreme top and right of the plot is 2301-2400 Saturday; it has the (joint) highest number of incidents (44 in total, or 0.8 per hour on the average occasion), and the highest number of patrol units dispatched (86 in total, or 1.6 per hour on the average occasion).

It is important to note that a patrol unit could range from one officer to a PSU.

Some points on the plot represent more than one hour of the weekend, since the hours in question have identical scores on both axes.

57

Figure 3

Number of arrests against number of incidents recorded each hour

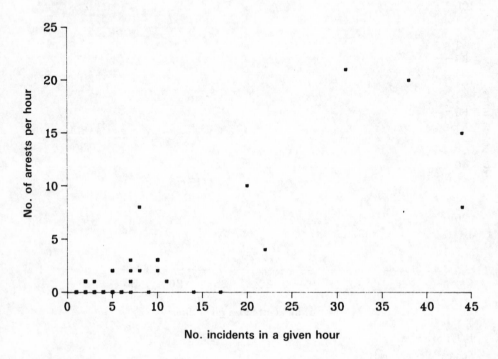

NOTES:

Source: message pads.

Number of incidents = 443.

The plot covers the period 0601 Friday morning to 2400 Sunday night. Each point on the plot represents one hour of this period, and has two scores. The horizontal axis shows the total number of public disorder incidents recorded over 9 weekends and 6 areas, the vertical axis the total number of people arrested in connection with these incidents.

The arrest score for each hour is therefore based on information from incidents accumulated during 54 'occasions', where an occasion equals a particular weekend in a particular area. Hence to obtain the average overall occasions for a given hour of the weekend, the total number of arrests for that hour, plotted above, should be divided by the 54 occasions on which it was based.

The incident score for each hour is accumulated in the same way, and the process is described in more detail on Figure 1.

The hours on this plot are not arranged in chronological order, but ranked according to their scores on each axis. The hour whose point is at the extreme top of the plot is 0001-0100 Sunday; it has the highest number of arrests (21 in total, or 0.4 per hour on the average occasion), but is ranked fourth in number of incidents (31 in total, or 0.6 per hour on the average occasion).

Some points on the plot represent more than one hour of the weekend, since the hours in question have identical scores on both axes.

that at these times the police (across the six towns for which the data were gathered) may be finding difficulty in responding in proportion to demand.

One possible explanation may be that officers, having made an arrest in the peak hour, are no longer available for dispatch in the hour after; another is that the police may find it difficult to roster enough officers for the hour after midnight because of the exigencies of the shift time.

The above analysis is open to query. As has already been explained above (page 56) a 'unit' is not a very clear measure of police strength. More work and fresh data would be required to test the tentative inference made here. But the analysis tends to validate the police view (as recorded in the press release on the ACPO report – see Chapter 1) that there is some difficulty in meeting calls created by disorder incidents late at night.

A similar analysis was made of the number of arrests made in any given hour, plotted against the numbers of calls for help in any given hour. It was established that there were more arrests made when the numbers of calls for help concerning disorder incidents was at a middling rate. When the number of calls for help per hour were heaviest, a lesser number of arrests were made. This suggests that when the incident rate is at its peak, police have difficulty in making arrests; either because crowds are too big to handle or because resources are spread too thinly. (See Figure 3.)

The main other finding of the message-pad analysis relevant to police deployment and tactics, is the fact already mentioned that a geographic mapping of incidents showed them to be extremely localised and many to be related to the 'cluster points' and, in particular, the 'congestion points' mentioned at Chapter 5, page 52. (Detailed maps are not reproduced in this report but are available to the police forces concerned.) Maps of the location of incidents provide a possible tool for predicting the focus of demand. To the extent that demand arises very clearly from specific sites and areas (and peaks at very narrowly specific times) it should be possible to meet it with economy. This argument must modify the case that resources may be over-taxed at certain points in time. Careful analytic planning based on where and how disorder arises on a particular weekend might help towards the accurate deployment of existing resources.

The Guildford and Woking surveys and group discussions

As described at page 4 and page 38, an important part of this study was a survey of the drinking patterns and experiences of disorder of young men using Guildford and Woking as entertainment centres.

As part of this survey, the young people were asked to name the most serious disorder incident they themselves had observed in the last year and to say whether or not the police were involved in it. Results were very similar across the two towns. 58% of Guildford respondents and 60% of Woking respondents said the police had been present and involved at the most serious disorder incident they had witnessed. But 31% of Guildford respondents and 30% of Woking respondents said the police had not been present (the remaining proportions of both samples – 12% in Guildford and 10% in Woking – were made up of 'Don't knows').

The young respondents were also asked whether they thought the police behaved 'fairly' or 'unfairly' to 'young people' out enjoying themselves in Guildford/Woking on Friday and Saturday nights. Once again results were similar across the two towns. 57% of Guildford respondents and 54% of Woking respondents thought the police did behave 'fairly'; 20% of Guildford respondents and 23% of Woking respondents thought they behaved 'unfairly'. The rest of each sample (24% in Guildford, 23% in Woking) recorded no view.

In the group discussions, held in both Guildford and Woking, a view emerged that the police in Woking were more heavy-handed than the police in Guildford. The survey data suggest that this view was not truly representative of the general view of the police in both towns. The observational and interview work (Chapter 3, page 24) had suggested that the Woking police in summer 1988 had been making a special effort to reduce the problems which had surfaced in the ACPO report for 1987 and had resulted in Woking being chosen as a 'trouble-site' for the study. These special efforts may have affected the views of the group (who were specially interested in and knowledgeable about street disorder). But the survey data show they had not had a general effect on the views of young people in Woking. The message-pad data suggests, if anything, that the Guildford police were the more 'heavy-handed', in that in 28% of drink-related incidents, the police themselves had initiated action rather than responding to a complaint relayed over the radio, and that in 38% of drink-related incidents an arrest had resulted. The corresponding figures for Woking were 9% and 23%.

The young men in the groups spent some time talking about the role of the police as disorder developed and complained both that the police sometimes aggravate a situation by taking unnecessarily strong action and that they sometimes waited too long to intervene, sitting back and allowing a fight to develop from a relatively small argument. The apparent contradiction of these two complaints shows the extreme delicacy of the police task. But perhaps the contradiction is more apparent than real. What the young people appear to be asking for is early firm action before the disorder develops and before it is necessary to come in in strength, thus possibly escalating an already difficult situation. This is still not an easy option, but not a totally contradictory one. The young men in the group discussions further suggested that older policemen and policewomen of any age were more likely to be able to 'talk down' potental disorder.

Most young men in the group discussions were in favour of more police action to reduce under-age drinking. They saw under-age drinking as a source or cause of violence. Strict control over entry was generally approved of for night-clubs and it was felt it could usefully be extended to pubs. In the words of the reporter on the group discussions:— "Drink was felt to be dangerous in the hands of under-age drinkers who were felt not to have the experience either to cope with large amounts of alcohol or with the social niceties of a Friday night in Woking". Both Woking and Guildford were said to have a lot of under-age drinking. It was claimed that some people used youngsters (eg under 16 year olds) to provoke fights by egging them on to make 'suicidal' comments and then stepping in to 'defend them'. The young men in these groups were broadly in favour of an identity card system, particularly for town-centre pubs, and had no objection in principle to the idea of such controls.

The observational and interview data

In all the six areas where observational fieldwork was carried out (see Chapter 3) fieldworkers carried out extensive interviews with police, a wide variety of court officials, probation officers and licensees. Their own observations of police practices at disorder incidents gave them further data to work on.

It is impossible to present all the rich material in full, but some particular insights and initiatives emerged, sometimes from several of the areas studied. They will be described under two headings: police strategies at management level, and police liaison with the licensed trade.

Police strategies at management level

Not unnaturally, most forces which had a disorder problem had worked hard to devise ways of defusing it. Strategies varied considerably, even across the mere six case-study areas. It seemed to the researchers that more could be done to monitor, record and exchange strategies across the whole of non-metropolitan England and Wales.

The findings of the present study are far too tentative and partial to attempt this in any authoritative way. But it seemed clear to the fieldworkers that those areas which had implemented an early reaction, early intervention strategy (notably Woking and Cowplain) were being the most successful in containing disorder. In Woking, the researchers were told that the Superintendent had introduced a policy that no officer must threaten to arrest without following through and that this had been felt to be effective. It has become the tactic of the police in Woking not to accept any form of verbal abuse. This is seen as unacceptable behaviour, not to be tolerated on duty or by the general public. To implement this policy the policeman needs to be very clear about his powers regarding arrests under Section 4 or Section 5 of the Public Order Act. Section 4 gives immediate powers of arrest, although Section 5 does not. Magistrates and youth workers in some other towns (not Woking) have suggested that lack of clarity among the police as to their powers results in arrested youngsters later being discharged. Cowplain police also seemed to follow a policy of relatively early intervention but commented that this needed expensive back-up. The Waterlooville centre is regularly patrolled and a personnel carrier parked there in the latter part of the evening.

However, the regular provision of back-up does not in itself seem sufficient to reduce disorder. One force, which had a continuing problem across its area, had initiated a system which was designed to provide operational assistance in exceptional circumstances throughout the five divisions in the county. In the early days of the system each division was able to raise a PSU within an hour with one inspector, two sergeants and up to twenty men. The way the system operated was that spotters would work in local towns and direct the PSU to any trouble. It seemed clear that the 'spotters' ie the beat constables, were not expected to intervene to defuse trouble *before* they called for the PSU.

Opinion among the police interviewed varied about the value of this strategy. Some felt it discouraged low-level early intervention and encouraged intervention too late and too heavily. Others felt that when the man on the scene knew he *could* call for reinforcements, he was more willing to seek an early intervention. It was the potential threat of things getting out of hand, as one officer put it, which necessitated the PSU back-up – it was a morale problem.

These are clearly difficult questions of police operational policy, which cannot be answered on the partial and superficial data provided here. This report can do no more than raise questions in police strategy. But common-sense suggests that if the real function of PSUs is simply to back up morale by providing a capability for early intervention, they need to be more accessible than an hour's drive away.

The fieldworkers in this study (and there were six of them; each of whom spent an intensive month observing, interviewing and thinking about the problem) were unanimously of the opinion that an early intervention strategy, which dealt firmly with initial signs of violence – such as public drunkenness, bad-mouthing the police, throwing glasses – was probably best. Where it was applied it seemed possible to prevent the build-up of street bacchanal to the state where any minor incident still needed heavy intervention – which in turn called forth heavy reaction. Yet the fieldworkers also clearly understood that in certain very disorderly areas, the 'rules of the game' had shifted so far that it would be foolhardy or impossible for single beat officers, or pairs of officers, to attempt early interventions. They, quite rightly, were too aware of the dangers of doing so. In such towns where public drunkenness, the taunting of the police and glass-throwing has become routine, it might, the fieldworkers felt, be necessary to have PSU back-up *closely* available (within 5 minutes) for the first few weeks in which a more stringent early intervention strategy was put into force.

The fieldworkers further observed that they felt a problem was caused by the timing of the police late-night shift. In most towns and entertainment centres, the pattern of evening disorder builds up slowly. A minor incident report from one particular pub early in the evening (for instance that a gang of lads are hunting for another) can build up to confrontations later at congestion sites. The whole pattern of events from about 6.30 pm to 1 am seemed to observers a continuous one. Yet, with some variations, the current practice standard within police forces, is for the Inspector in charge of a shift to change over at 10 pm, along with all his officers. For an hour before the shift changes, police are gradually drifting back to the station. For an hour after it, the new staff are being briefed and are not yet out in force. The briefings observed were reasonably casual affairs and rarely involved more specific instructions than "we've got a few gobby yobs out there; look out for them". As one observer put it, changing the man in charge of policing order in the middle of a weekend drinking evening is "rather like switching air-traffic controllers at Heathrow at peak hours". Ideally attempts should be made to provide greater continuity of cover before, during, and after the peak trouble times. Without making a major change in shift patterns, it should be possible to give the early evening shift two hours overtime and to adjust supervision arrangements, so that one inspector was responsible for policing for the entire evening and the number of officers available between 10 pm and midnight was maximised. The cost of two hours overtime on Friday and Saturday evenings for a limited number of officers is likely to be a good deal less than a significant increase in police manpower. It could be scheduled in advance on a regular basis, which would keep costs down. These ideas are simply the thoughtful reflections of interested observers. The police themselves (and the Inspectorate) will have far more data accessible to them to solve these problems. But the observers' insights are worth recording since they raise interesting questions and suggest useful areas for future consideration if we are to learn how to deal with problems of disorder.

Police liaison with the licensed trade

In several of the areas studied particular police strategies were in hand to liaise with the local licensed trade. Sudbury had a 'Pub Watch' scheme in which local publicans and the police co-operated to pass messages between them by telephone about any troublesome groups of drinkers. The police in Gravesend also put a lot of effort into relations with licensees. There is some interest in initiatives such as that pioneered in Brighton in which the police in co-operation with licensees attempt to police under-age drinking more successfully. (The evidence of our survey, page 46, suggests that about a third of 16 and 17 year olds drink regularly in pubs on Friday or Saturday.) The under-age drinking rule is notoriously difficult to enforce given the fact that it is hard to tell young people's age on sight and that many publicans still believe that an honest misperception of a customer's age is a sufficient defence in law to this offence. (In fact, the 1988 Licensing Act shifted the burden of proof substantially on to the licensee.)

One way of tackling the problem of under-age drinking would be of course to demand ID cards. There is some ambivalence as to the likely usefulness of this scheme. It would certainly seem to be a way of enforcing laws against under-age drinking; but given the high proportion of this age-group likely to be out on the streets on Friday or Saturday night, there could be some displacement of disorder effects. The likely usefulness of rules against drinking in the streets (eg 'The Coventry bye-law') were not considered in this study. They are the topic of separate research by the Home Office.

Discussion and summary

This chapter has described data from police message pads, from surveys and group discussions and from observations; all of which bear on the difficult questions of police operational policy concerning violence.

The question of whether more financial resources are needed to deal with this undoubted problem is not easy to answer. Analysis of the message-pad data suggested that resources may indeed be putting a constraint on ability to respond in strength after midnight or to arrest at peak hours (although the finding can be no more than tentative). On the opposite side it could be argued that the very predictability of possible public order offences in terms of time and location (peaking at 'congestion' sites which can clearly be mapped) should make them easier to contain with careful forward planning. It was suggested that more work needed to be done to devise the best policing methods to handle and control the weekend violence and it was suggested that the most successful method seemed to be early low level intervention to prevent signs of public violence and disorder escalating, rather than late intervention in strength. In towns where matters had already got out of hand, with habitual police-taunting and baiting, it may be necessary to have good support within easy and rapid reach of beat officers until habits of order are re-established.

The possible usefulness of identity cards as a means of reducing drinking was brought up in group discussions and aroused no strong objections. The group discussion participants were in favour of stronger action against under-age drinking. The question of ID cards is not of course solely one for the police and is discussed further in the concluding chapter (page 68).

A final point stressed by observers was the need for clarity as to the goals of policing in entertainment centres. Was the goal simply to clear the streets as soon as possible after closing hours? Or should the objective be to allow the young people to congregate and party on the streets and outside the take-aways, so long as no overt violence or drunkenness occurred? Something must depend on local residents. Where an entertainment centre is also a residential area, where people are trying to sleep, it may be difficult to follow the latter policy. But where the entertainment is in an area of shops and offices, the latter policy may be the correct one. Whatever the policy to be followed it should be clear to citizens, the young people and the police themselves.

7 Summary and Discussion

The ACPO report, the results of which were made public in June 1988, gave rise to wide public concern. It established that the police were experiencing problems in policing disorder in non-metropolitan areas, especially disorder relating to alcohol consumption. Throughout the summer of 1988 both press and TV were full of accounts of 'rural violence' and of 'lager louts'. The phrase 'rural violence' was an especially emotive one. It created a picture of mythical, tranquil rural England, that green and pleasant land, suddenly prey to forms of mob violence and loutishness which had been thought to belong essentially to the corrupt city. The ACPO report called for more detailed study to understand the nature of the phenomenon it recorded. The Home Secretary announced it would be carried out. This report records that research.

The first point to emerge is that the phenomenon cannot accurately be described as 'rural violence'. The incidents recorded by the ACPO came from 'non-metropolitan areas' and as Map 1, Chapter 1 shows, non-metropolitan England and Wales is a very wide area indeed. It does indeed include the whole of rural England and Wales, but it also includes major cities such as Oxford, Nottingham, Plymouth, Brighton, Colchester, Stratford-on-Avon and those great swathes of prosperous, densely settled, semi-rural semi-urban areas so characteristic of the prosperous South-East. Areas such as the Slough triangle, the Medway towns, the Thames Valley, Havant, can no longer reasonably be described simply as 'rural'. They are among the most densely settled areas in Europe.

Chapter 2 of this study describes a 'locational analysis' of the 251 incidents which occurred in England and Wales in 1987 and were recorded in the ACPO report. No less than 118 of these incidents came from areas classified as 'mixed town and country with some industry' or 'higher status growth areas', another 34 came from cities or traditional manufacturing areas, 23 from commuting or suburban areas, 15 from seaside resort or retirement areas. Only 58 came from genuine 'more rural areas'; this despite the fact that the criteria for inclusion in the ACPO report list included 'difficulty in bringing up police reinforcements' which would tend to bias the list to include more disorder incidents in remote areas.

Inevitably, many of the high-growth, mixed town and country areas where non-metropolitan disorder occurred are in the South of England. The North of England is more characteristically divided into metropolitan areas of traditional heavy manufacturing and more remote rural areas. It is not surprising that the 'non-metropolitan' incidents mapped by ACPO cluster in the south.

In order to describe the nature of incidents of disorder or violence, three paired sites were selected for further study; one of each pair a major 'trouble-site' in the

65

ACPO data, the other as near as possible a match in terms of socio-demographic variables. Chapter 3 describes the kind of disorder found in the three pairs of sites studied. Contrary to expectation, disorder was as prevalent in some of the 'control' or 'matched' sites as in the selected 'trouble-sites'; and the position in some 'trouble-site' towns had improved between 1987 (when the ACPO data originated) and the summer of 1988 (when this study was carried out). It seems that the possibility of disorder is latent in many of the areas selected by our locational analysis.

Whether such disorder erupts in one particular town, village, or entertainment centre rather than another appears to depend on a complex amalgam of reasons including the history and reputation of the place, the size or sudden growth of the young male population, the siting and geography of entertainment and fast-food outlets and the success or otherwise of the police in setting reasonably orderly 'rules of the game'.

Both in Chapter 3 and Chapter 4 some accounts were given of the typical weekend drinking habits of the young. Disorder is not so much found in licensed outlets themselves, but in the streets afterwards. Young people leave pubs en masse at the same hour, emerge on to the streets still looking for further entertainment, cluster at fast-food outlets or at other gathering points and are at this point excitable tinder, ready for any spark which may cause quarrels or violence. Both the survey and group discussion data presented at Chapter 4 showed that weekend drinking (sometimes quite heavy drinking) is a routine social habit among the young. Even among 16 to 17 year olds resident in typical entertainment centres, a third are using the pubs on a Friday or Saturday night. "Going out to the pub" is quite simply what young people do on a weekend evening, to meet others and to enjoy themselves.

Only a minority of these youngsters become participants in disorder and/or violence. Is there anything to distinguish participants from observers and non-participants? This question is discussed in Chapter 4 and it is shown that participants in disorder are more likely to have unskilled jobs or to be unemployed (the group discussions suggest sometimes voluntarily) and to have left school at sixteen. These are young men who have not yet found their role in society. They may not have enough money to go on to night-clubs after their evening in the pub (even if they exist in their vicinity); they cluster outside take-aways, unwilling for the evening to end, still looking for excitement. It is these gatherings which are the characteristic focus of disorder. Since it is often said that a spell in the armed services might be good for possible trouble-makers, it is worth noting that 'squaddies' or soldiers are often said to be the source of trouble.

Some possible strategies for prevention are discussed in Chapter 5, which concentrates on entertainment patterns and in Chapter 6 which concentrates on the role of police. At Chapter 5, it is suggested more could be done by planning authorities, brewery managers and managers of fast-food chains to control the siting of outlets so 'congestion sites' are not created. It is also suggested that the 'disco pub' or 'youth pub' may be a particular source of excitement and that perhaps consideration should be given to changing the rules under which these establishments operate. At present they are far less controlled than establishments with late-night music and dancing licences.

The discussion of police strategies at Chapter 6 makes clear the extreme difficulty of the police task. There is some tentative evidence that they may have difficulty in responding in proportionate strength to disorder incidents in the hour or so after pub closing. But it is argued that the most successful strategy appears to be early intervention at a low level before really excitable and disorderly crowds build up, rather than late intervention in strength. In areas where 'the rules of the game' have already become very lax and even early intervention would be difficult without back-up, such back-up could possibly be provided on a temporary basis until the habits of orderly public behaviour are re-established. The group discussions suggest that such early intervention strategies might not be unpopular with the mass of young people. It was further observed that problems are caused for the police by the switch in shift in the middle of Friday and Saturday evenings; this makes it difficult for a total police operation over the whole evening to be closely planned.

It is stressed that these suggestions for police strategy are inevitably tentative, based as they are on one month's observations and discussions. The police themselves have a great wealth of experience in these matters. They have successfully policed the traditional Friday night and Saturday night pub crawls and heavy drinking of Northern industrial towns for generations. The present study suggests that they have already developed expertise and techniques, in areas such as Cowplain and Woking, which can be successful in dealing with areas which had become very troublesome. There need to be more detailed case studies and exchanges of information and techniques as to how to deal with this classic and difficult problem, which is essentially a problem of policing entertainment centres.

Patterns of weekend drinking

But the problem of non-metropolitan disorder is not one with which the police alone can be expected to deal. This report has shown that most of these disorderly incidents are intimately connected with the drinking patterns of the young and with patterns of pub-going at the weekend. Some incidents fall outside this pattern – the disturbance at a suburban party; the incident away from normal entertainment centre gathering points – but both police message pads and observational data show that the majority of disorderly incidents are connected with weekend entertainment patterns.

This British pattern of weekend entertainment drinking is not a new pattern; nor is it likely quickly to change. As one senior police inspector, with experience in North of England towns in the fifties and sixties, observed during the course of this study – "Surely 'twas ever thus". The new salience of the problem of entertainment centre disorder is that it is not now a feature solely of industrial areas or large entertainment centres. Movements of work, of population, of prosperity, mean that similar patterns of drinking and entertainment have spread to newly prosperous and populated areas, including those in the South of England, still thought of as 'the country'.

Possible policy initiatives

Any solution of the problem is thus at least as much a matter for social policy
generally as it is for the police. Several useful reports have recently been published
on alcohol policy and many useful initiatives have been put in hand. Not all will
be discussed here, but a few, particularly relevant to the disorder problem, will be
briefly discussed:—

(a) *Reducing alcohol consumption by the young*

Many have argued that the major need is to reduce alcohol consumption,
particularly by young males. But this report has reminded us of the centrality
of 'going out to the pub' in the life of young people. Whatever the price of beer
it is unlikely that youngsters will stop the habit of Friday and Saturday nights
out. The pub is where they meet their friends; going to the pub is a mass social
habit. The quickest and most effective strategy to reduce alcohol consumption
among this age group would probably be to ensure that lower alcohol drinks (and
non-alcoholic drinks) were more freely available in pubs; and more fashionable.
Low alcohol and non-alcohol beers need both to be cheaper and to have a more
acceptable image for youngsters out for a night on the town. It is encouraging
that the brewing industry have of late been doing more to promote them.

(b) *Staggered closing hours*

Another initiative which could be useful is somehow to stagger pub-closing
times. The mass ejection of excited young drinkers on to crowded streets and
to crowded take-aways, at precisely the same time, is obviously a large part of
the disorder problem in this country. It does not happen in France and Germany
which allow late-night opening – and which have far less of a disorder problem.
But this is admittedly a difficult question. Many would fear that longer opening
times would result in more alcohol consumption with accompanying health
problems. The results of the recent liberalisation of licensing law to allow the
opening at all hours up to 11 pm may well be relevant to this question.

(c) *Identity cards and the prevention of under-age drinking*

This study has established that there is a substantial problem of under-age
drinking in this country (page 40 Chapter 4) and that under-age drinkers are
more likely than older ones to be involved in disorder (page 41). Any strategy
to reduce under-age drinking would therefore seem to show promise of reducing
disorder. One strategy which has recently become prominent is for proprietors
of licensed premises to demand identity cards from youngsters before serving
them with alcoholic drinks, in order to ensure that the law is not being broken.
(The law allows 16 and 17 year olds to be in a pub, but prohibits them from
ordering or consuming alcoholic drinks while on the premises.) The young men
involved in the group discussions in this study were on the whole in favour of
identity cards as a way of tightening up the observance of under-age drinking
laws (page 60). Local experiments and initiatives in the use of ID cards in pubs
are in place in many areas and the effects of those schemes should be monitored.

Identity cards may not be the most successful strategy to enforce the law. It is possible their effect could be circumvented, for instance by persuading older members of a given drinking group to buy alcoholic drinks at the bar. It is possible that if they did work and 16 and 17 year olds ceased to visit pubs, their anti-social activities would simply displace elsewhere, less easy to police. In Guildford and Woking one third of the young men aged 16-17 were using pubs at the weekend. This is a lot of young men to have wandering the sreets or looking for entertainment elsewhere. If they are not to resort to warehouse parties or drinking in derelict buildings, any strict enforcement of the law needs to be accompanied at local level with a serious attempt to provide alternative places of resort.

As this report has stressed, the precise determinants of disorder vary considerably at local level. For these reasons it would seem best that each local area to work out its own policies for applying the law on under-age drinking.

More general strategies: the brewing interest

The strategies suggested so far depend in some way on legislative or fiscal controls. But there is much that citizens themselves can do to ameliorate the problems of non-metropolitan violence, within the current legislative and fiscal framework. Action is possible on two fronts: both by the brewing industry and by the public.

A recent market research report prepared for the brewing industry ('The On Trade Revolution', Mintel Publications Ltd, 1988) has shown that more than £13 billion passed across the counters of pubs and other licensed premises in 1987 but that alcoholic drinks accounted for only two thirds of this turnover and that this proportion is shrinking. More and more turnover (and profits) are coming from the sale of food and non-alcoholic drinks. The Mintel report argues that, if the profitability of the industry is to be sustained, the historic male-dominated pub-culture forbidding to women and families must change. They forecast that food and soft drinks are the growth section of the market and will overtake alcohol as the biggest source of revenue for the on-trade within the next five years. The report says "Pub culture has historically been a male one, largely community based and implicitly forbidding to women and families. Pub owners can no longer afford to rely on their historical customer base". The image of the pub as primarily somewhere for young men to 'knock back lager' in Saturday night sessions is now irrelevant to the industry as a whole, Mintel believes.

If Mintel are right, it is in the interest of the licensed trade itself, as well as of society as a whole, to get rid of the image of the pub as a haunt for 'lager louts', a place of danger and disorder. It may be tempting for large tied house chains to retain some 'rough pubs' in central entertainment locations taking quick profits from the high-spending heavy-drinking youth market. But it is dangerous for the trade as a whole to ignore the impact such pubs have on the perceptions and social habits of the wider market. Most British pubs are not 'free houses', they are tied outlets, the responsibility of large brewing chains. The large brewery chains have already done much but could perhaps do more to civilise the 'youth pubs' in central entertainment locations, by making sure there is enough space, by making sure food and non-alcoholic drinks are more easily available, and by encouraging the presence of young women.

More general strategies: the public

Finally, is there anything the concerned citizen can do in places plagued by entertainment centre violence? This report suggests there is and can be. Towns known as 'trouble-sites' *can* turn round and become more civilised places on Friday and Saturday evenings. The young men who cause the disorder do not seem, by and large, to be actuated by any particular aggressive principles. They are mainly bored youngsters with nowhere to go, who may have drunk too much and are looking for entertainment. Disorder escalates sporadically, almost by accident, much influenced by the direct physical situation.

When any particular town, village or area becomes known as a trouble-site, local interests should come together to consider just what are determinants of the local problem and what steps could be taken to reduce it. Are, for instance, the take-aways sited in the wrong place? Is there insufficient transport away from the city centre? Where do incidents map? At what time? Would for instance a late-night coffee stall at the other end of town be a useful initiative? Could someone be found to staff it?

The exact problems to be solved will differ in each place but earlier chapters of the report suggest both means of analysis of local disorder and ways of improving matters. It could be useful in any area known to be the site of trouble for citizens to join together with the divisional Police Commander and local authority representatives to attempt to work out what could be done. Local police/community consultative groups could well take the lead in initiating discussion. Licensees and proprietors of take-aways should be represented on any committee. And, most importantly, the young people themselves who use the local entertainment centre should be consulted. Some of them will have pursued violence, but the great majority are not seeking violence; they are seeking a happy night out with their friends. Their insights as to how to prevent violence and disorder could be more useful than anyone else's.

The smaller towns and entertainment centres of England and Wales are not without social resources and social cohesion. A problem has been identified – first by the ACPO report and now by this study. The citizens of non-metropolitan England and Wales can do a great deal to solve it.

70

Drinking and Disorder: Appendices

Index of Appendices

References

Association of Chief Police Officers. (1988). *Public Disorder Outside Metropolitan Areas – An ACPO Study.* Surrey Constabulary.

Ashley, K. M. (1984). *A Study of Disorder in Sunderland Town Centre.* Executive Summary. Northumbria Police.

Craig, J. (1981). *A 1981 Socio-economic Classification of Local Health Authorities of Great Britain.* Studies of Medical and Population Subjects No. 48. London: HMSO.

Ekblom, P. and Heal, K. (1982). *The Police response to calls from the public.* Research and Planning Unit Paper No. 9. London: Home Office.

Goddard, E. and Ikin, C. (1988). *Drinking in England and Wales in 1987.* London: HMSO.

Hope, T. J. (1985). 'Drinking and disorder in the city centre: a policy analysis'. In Hope, T. J. *Implementing Crime Prevention Measures.* Home Office Research Study no. 86. London: HMSO.

Mintel Publications Ltd. (1988). *The On Trade Revolution.*

Ramsay, M. (1982). *City-Centre Crime: The Scope For Situational Prevention.* Research and Planning Unit Paper No. 10. London: Home Office.

Central Statistical Office. *Regional Trends 22.* (1987). London: HMSO.

Appendix A: Descriptions of 'families' and 'clusters' together with Tables for Chapter 2

Descriptions of families and clusters.

At Chapter 2 of this study, the incidents listed in the ACPO report of 1988 on 'Public Disorder outside Metropolitan Areas' are analysed by their location in various 'family' or 'cluster' areas. The following extract from Craig, J. A. (1981) *A socio-economic classification of Local Health Authorities of Great Britain* gives details of these 'family' or 'cluster' areas:—

Family 1A: Established high status areas

This family consists of three clusters; it contains 59 districts and 14 per cent of the GB population. Geographically the family is concentrated in the South East, where it includes many of the established commuter districts surrounding London as well as several outer London boroughs. Equivalent districts for several other large conurbations and cities are also included although these are fewer in number.

This family has the highest social class structure of all the families. The age structure is also significant because the 45-64s are markedly over-represented and children are under-represented with the youngest children being the most under-represented; probably because couples move into these areas as their children are growing up. Moreover there is also a tendency to move out on retirement; the proportion of over 65s is a little below average which contrasts with the much above average proportion of 45-64s. However, rate of inflow is low and the 'changes of address in previous year' were markedly less than for any other family apart from Family 3 *(mixed areas with some industry)*. This low rate is especially remarkable because the proportion of owner-occupiers was high.

Unemployment was low and the proportion of students was high; two-car households were relatively common although exceeded by Family 1B *(higher status growth areas)*. This latter fact being more an indication of a difference in life-style than a comparision of affluence – for example, the greater amount of commuting by rail in this family than in Family 1B. The proportion of New Commonwealth-born people in the population is higher than in many families but this is probably largely due to the concentration of the family in the South East of England.

The number of persons per household was about average and rooms per household were somewhat above average. Amenities were good but not outstanding. All of which is a reminder that although these are, overall, high status areas nevertheless the districts are still mixed. Thus 18 per cent of the population were still in the semi-skilled or unskilled category – less than the national average of 25 per cent, or the 29 per cent in Family 4, but still an appreciable proportion.

Clusters of Family 1A (C1-C3)

The three clusters are of a large easily distinguished character. *Cluster 1* consists of high class centres popular with commuters but some distance from London (such as Sevenoaks, Guildford, Chiltern, St Albans) *together* with some areas of an equivalent status from other parts of the country: Macclesfield in Cheshire, Beverley in Humberside, and two suburbs of Glasgow (Bearsden and Milngavie, Eastwood). Whereas *Cluster 3* consists of nine prestigous outer London boroughs together with Epsom and Ewell from Surrey. The other, *Cluster 2*, is more of a mixture and consists of four other outer London boroughs and several shorter distance commuting districts which like Epsom and Ewell, and unlike the areas in Cluster 1, are contiguous to London. In addition Cluster 2 contains many more areas from outside London which are essentially suburban in character. Thus Gedling has this kind of connection with Nottingham; Fareham with Portsmouth and Southampton; Warwick, and Rugby, with the West Midlands; Sefton with Merseyside; and so on.

The family as a whole has a high social class profile and Cluster 1 has the highest profile; it also has a high proportion of large houses, two-car households and so on. Cluster 2 is more evenly balanced between services and manufacturing employment (both are about the national average) and has not such an extreme social structure as Clusters 1 or 3. Also there is less rented accommodation and the age structure is closer to the national average except for a shortfall of over 65s. For Cluster 3 certain housing indicators stand out: more furnished letting and shared amenities together with more single person, non-pensioner, households. Public transport to work is more common and the New Commonwealth-born population is about twice the national average (compared with a half in Cluster 1). The services-manufacturing employment split is strongly towards services.

Family 1B: Higher status growth areas

This family consists of two clusters, it contains 47 districts and 9 per cent of Great Britain's population. Over half the districts are in the outer parts of the South East region; there are none in Scotland, the North or Yorkshire and Humberside regions. The districts occur only in the regions which are more populated *and* more prosperous.

This is a fairly distinctive family – it has a very young age structure with fewer over-45s, and more children than any other family. The social class structure is high, though not so high as Family 1A *(established high status areas)*, and the service industries were less important: similarly owner-occupation is above average but not the highest. However, the proportion of two-car households was the highest of all families and the use of public transport low. Unemployment was low. The population includes a large proportion of children so the number of persons per household was high; but the number of rooms per household was also high, and large (four and more children) families were uncommon – hence overcrowding was rare. There were few one person households.

Because these are growth areas it might be expected that the number of changes of address in the previous year would be high. But, though above the national average, there were several other families with higher rates. Family 6b *(Central*

74

London) is much the highest but Family 2A *(more rural areas)* and Family 2B *(resort and retirement areas)* also had higher rates. The probable explanation is that once settled the population are less prone to move than in places where there are more young single people or old people.

Clusters of Family 1B (C4-C5)

The two clusters are fairly equal in size and both have a minority of districts from outside the South East. The sharpest distinction between the two is that *Cluster 5* has a higher proportion of people in manufacturing, and fewer in agriculture and services, than does *Cluster 4*. Overall Cluster 5 is rather more urban and also of lower social status; and has the younger age structure. There is also less rented accommodation in Cluster 5 and fewer large houses or two-car households.

Family 2A: More rural areas

This family is a large one and contains 106 districts – nearly one quarter of all the districts of Great Britain but a smaller proportion (12 per cent) of the population. The family is made up of four clusters. The districts are spread throughout Great Britain although they are most common in the South West, East Anglia, northern England, and Scotland, in each of these areas nearly half the districts belong to this family. Conversely there are very few of these districts in the Liverpool-London axial belt.

The most distinctive feature of the family is the high proportion of the working population employed in agriculture: 8.6 per cent compared with a national average of 2.1 per cent. The mixed social structure of the population is also quite different to any other family as is the household tenure structure. The age structure is rather elderly but the number of persons per household is about average with few single non-pensioner households. The proportion of address changes was high and the New Commonwealth-born people were rarer than in any other family.

Clusters of Family 2A (C6-C9)

Clusters 7 and *8* contain the remoter, more agricultural areas respectively north and south of the Scottish border; such areas in Scotland are differentiated from those in England or Wales because Scottish housing conditions are so different. *Cluster 8* consists of much of Wales, much of the South West, several districts around or near the Wash and the districts straddling the Pennines in northern England. Rural, agricultural, districts also make up *Cluster 9* but these latter districts mostly consist of a well-known medium-size town which serves as a centre for the surrounding rural hinterland and indeed often for further afield (for example, Chester, Chichester, Harrogate, Winchester). This distinguishes them from Cluster 8; in the latter the towns are smaller and less well-known so that the districts are more wholly dependent on agriculture and related activities.

Cluster 6 also consists of rural districts – but of ones with a difference. Several have a large Armed Forces establishment within their boundaries with populations large enough to affect the overall age and employment structure, housing variables and so on. Thus Richmondshire (with Catterick Camp) and Rushmoor (with Aldershot) are included. There are also four areas in north-east Scotland (Gordon, Moray, Ross and Cromarty, Shetland Islands) where it is oil-related growth that has led to a similar influx of a young, and often transitory population. And the districts in this cluster are not especially similar to one another – as is shown by the distances from the centroid and from the list of most similar districts. What they have in common is the negative characteristic that they are rural areas with peculiar population structures.

Family 2B: Resort and retirement areas

This family consists of a single cluster *(Cluster 10)* containing 29 districts and 5 per cent of the population. The districts are on the south coast with a few elsewhere (for example, North Wales, Blackpool, Scarborough, Southend-on-Sea, and so on).

This is one of the more distinctive families. Its most striking feature is its age structure; the proportion of children is well below that in any other family except Family 6B and the over 65s are more numerous. The average number of persons per household is low but dwellings are of average size – so overcrowding is also low. The proportion of owner-occupiers is higher than for any other family including Family 1A *(established high status areas)* – and the proportion of tenants (council and housing association) is least. There is an above average proportion of rented accommodation.

The social class structure is higher than average but not so much so as either Family 1A or 1B. The industrial structure is strongly inclined towards services and away from manufacturing; unemployment was about average. There were relatively few students or New Commonwealth-born; the numbers of persons changing address was above average.

Family 3:   Mixed, town and country, areas with some industry

This family is the largest of all the families – 108 districts and no less than 22 per cent of the population. It consists of four clusters. The districts are amongst the most mixed in Great Britain and ofter include an older industrial centre together with an area of adjacent countryside. The bringing together of such areas was one of the deliberate aims of the reorganisation of local authority areas in the early 1970s, and it is interesting and useful that the classification picks out these districts as a distinct family. Of course, to an extent, all districts outside the largest conurbations are mixed for even the most rural will contain small towns and some industry. What distinguishes the districts in Family 3 is that the industry is more important and that the urban population usually exceeds the rural population – although the latter is still sufficiently large to influence the overall character of a district.

The family is by no means evenly spread over Great Britain and is most strongly represented in the older industrial areas. Thus Wales, East Midlands and North regions have about one half or more of their districts in this family; Yorkshire and Humberside, East Anglia and West Midlands have approaching one third or more.

Scotland has no districts in this family as its more industrial districts are allocated to Family 5. The family is, overall, the most typical of Great Britain as a whole and has similarities to Families 1, 2, 4. The proportion of the population employed in services is least of all the families; the social structure is biased, moderately, to the lower end of the scale although there is an especially large proportion of skilled manual workers. Housing tenure is fairly average and dwelling size is above average, but amenities are below average. The population's age structure is moderately young. Changes of address were very few and there were few students. There were also few New Commonwealth-born people – about the same as in Family 2 and not nearly so many as in Families 4-6.

Clusters of Family 3(C11-C14)
As mentioned above this is the most average family and has similarities with several of the other families. This is evident in each of its four clusters. *Cluster 11 (more rural areas with industry)* has something in common with Family 2A; indeed the level of employment in agriculture is twice the national average, and only a little below that in Clusters 6 and 9 (where agricultural areas were combined with towns which were important service centres, or included large Armed Forces establishments, and so on). But in Cluster 11 the combination is more with small manufacturing and industrial localities – for example, Kettering, Selby, Stroud, Yeovil are included. This cluster has more unfurnished rented accommodation, more large houses, and more two-car households than the rest of the family.

Cluster 13 contrasts with Cluster 11 in that the manufacturing and industrial sector is much more dominant and most districts include fair-sized traditional industrial towns – though again usually including some rural hinterland – Doncaster, Llanelli, Stoke-on-Trent and so on. The social class structure is a little below average and the proportion of local authority tenants is above average. Compared with Cluster 11 there are fewer two-car households, more travel to work by public transport, more unemployment and so on. Houses and flats are of average size but there are few very large or very small ones; the age structure of the population is near average except for a shortfall of over 65s.

Cluster 14 can be regarded as a very small offshoot of Cluster 13. It consists of three adjoining districts in South Wales which are evidently distinctive enough to form their own cluster. Particularly marked features include a more imbalanced social class structure, a very high level of poor amenities, few two-vehicle households, and few changes of address.

The remaining cluster in the family, *Cluster 12*, can be thought of as being between Clusters 11 and 13. For though Cluster 12 includes districts which are a mixture of town and country, the towns, though no smaller than those of Cluster 13, are not so industrial and have a larger service sector: for example, Carlisle, Cleethorpes, Northampton, Swansea. The social structure is balanced but the age structure is inclined towards the younger ages and there are rather more single, non-pensioner households, more furnished accommodation, and more shared amenities than in the rest of the family. But compared with Great Britain as a whole this cluster is, in most respects, close to the average.

Family 4A: Traditional manufacturing areas
This consists of two clusters. It contains 22 districts and 10 per cent of the population (and has little overlap with Family 4A in the 1971 classification). Many of the areas in Family 3 included a substantial rural or suburban hinterland; this is much less so for Family 4 and to some extent the classification is a reflection of the overbounding and underbounding of different cities. The family includes the bigger manufacturing centres in the Midlands, (Birmingham, Coventry, Wolverhampton), in Yorkshire (Bradford) and in the traditional textile towns of Lancashire (Oldham, Blackburn and others). The family does not occur in the more rural regions.

There is a high proportion of the work force in manufacturing and a high proportion of semi-skilled workers; a relatively large proportion of the married women work. The proportions of owner-occupiers and local authority tenants are close to the national average although the owner-occupied housing is of mixed quality and the proportion of households with no inside WC is high. There are few large houses. The age structure of the population is relatively young and large families are much more frequent than in any other family; there is a large New Commonwealth-born population – exceeded only by the two London families (6A and 6B).

Clusters of Family 4A (C15 and C16)
Of the two clusters, *Cluster 15* consists of five districts – three of which make up the industrial centre of the West Midlands (Birmingham, Sandwell and Wolver-hampton). Also included are Leicester and the East London borough of Newham. *Cluster 16* is larger and consists of Coventry and Derby from the Midlands, Luton and Waltham Forest from the South East, and with one exception (Western Isles), 12 other districts from Yorkshire and Lancashire (such as Bolton, Bradford and Preston).

The chief differences between the two clusters are that there is more local authority housing in Cluster 15 and housing conditions are worse: more overcrowding, more sharing amenities and more without an inside WC. Also the social structure is more unbalanced for Cluster 15 and the New Commonwealth-born population is larger – especially that from the African New Commonwealth.

Family 4B: Service centres and cities
This family consists of three clusters and contains 34 districts and 14 per cent of the population. The regions where the family is most common are the North and Yorkshire and Humberside regions; but some towns from the southern half of England are included. There are no districts in the West Midlands – although that region had several in Family 4A – and few in Wales or Scotland.

The family has a below average proportion of the workforce employed in manufacturing and an above average proportion in the service industries. At the same time the social structure has a marked deficit of professional and managerial households and a surplus of unskilled households. The housing tenure mix is inclined towards local authority tenants and away from owner-occupiers; the level of amenities is better than that for Family 4A (*traditional manufacturing areas*) or Family 3 (*mixed areas with some industry*) but not so high as in Families 1 or 2.

The age structure of the population shows a deficit of children and their parents (the 25-44s) but above average proportions for the other ages especially 15-24s, which is presumably due partly to students and partly to younger people starting work. Single person, non-pensioner, households and migrants are, correspondingly, above average. The New Commonwealth-born population is not, relatively, so large as in Family 4A but greater than in Families 3 or 5. Except Family 6 (*Inner and Central London*), this family has the lowest proportion of two-car households and the highest proportion of journeys to work by public transport.

Clusters of Family 4B (C17-C19)
Clusters 17 and 19 both contain a sizeable number of districts whereas Cluster 18 is another small cluster (only 3 districts). Hence the main contrast is between *Cluster 17*, which contains many of the larger cities such as Liverpool, Newcastle-upon-Tyne and Sheffield, and *Cluster 19*, which includes many of the less industrial regional centres of England (such as Bristol, Oxford, Reading and York). As with Family 4A these are districts which do not include much of the surrounding hinterland and their boundaries are usually little different from the old county boroughs. Cities for which the boundaries were extended tend to be in districts classified to Family 3.

Cluster 17 is more orientated to manufacturing, and less towards services, than Cluster 19, and the social class structure is accordingly more imbalanced. And the proportion of local authority tenants is well above average. Whereas for Cluster 19 they are about average. Cluster 19 does have, however, a lot of furnished accommodation. Age structures for all three clusters are much the same – slightly inclined toward the elderly but with an excess of 15-24s.

The three districts which make up *Cluster 18* are the cities of Edinburgh and Aberdeen together with Greenwich LB. The social class, age structure and household size are much as for both Clusters 17 and 19; however, the housing tenure pattern is more like Cluster 17's than Cluster 18's. But there are fewer large houses and more overcrowding though the sharing of amenities is less common. It is in these housing-related characteristics that the cluster is different.

Family 5: Areas with much local authority housing
This family consists of 5 clusters, which is more than any other family. It contains 38 districts and 8 per cent of the population. What the districts have in common is a very high proportion of local authority housing. In Scotland this occurs in many of the areas with predominantly urban populations; in England or Wales it is rarer and occurs in the New Towns and some inner London boroughs. Hence two thirds of the districts in this family are in Scotland and make up two almost wholly Scottish clusters; two of the clusters are almost wholly English and are centred on

new town developments; and the remaining cluster is an exceptional one consisting of Tower Hamlets and Glasgow.

As its name indicates, the family (and all its clusters) have a far higher proportion of local authority tenants than average; the national average is 33 per cent whereas this family has nearly twice that proportion. Accompanying this tenure pattern is a high level of amenities but few large dwellings. Households are the largest of all the families – so the crowding indicators are high. The age structure is young with many children and few older people; the social structure is the lowest of any family.

Clusters of Family 5 (C20-C24)
These five clusters highlight some of the differences within the family. The two largest clusters (C22 and C23) almost wholly consists of Scottish districts. *Cluster 22* contains eight districts from the heart of the Clyde-Forth industrial belt (and Knowsley from Merseyside) while *Cluster 23* consists of seventeen districts many of which are on the periphery of that belt. *Cluster 22* is the rather more industrial in that manufacturing employment is more important and the social class imbalance is greater; there is also a greater ratio of local authority tenants to owner-occupiers than for any of the twenty-eight clusters. Conversely *Cluster 23* is rather less extreme than *Cluster 22* and includes several districts which have towns that are centres in their own right such as Dundee, Falkirk and Renfrew.

Cluster 24 consists of just Glasgow and the London borough of Tower Hamlets. In 1971 Glasgow was distinctive enough and large enough to form a one-area cluster; this time it has been joined by Tower Hamlets although the similarity is not very great and both are unusual areas. They both have a very extreme social class structure; there is not quite so much local authority housing as in Cluster 22 but more rented accommodation and even fewer owner-occupiers. There seems to be a mixture of large and small households so that although the overall household size is about average, and the age structure is also average, there is a lot of overcrowding and shared amenities. There are very few two-car households and a high rate of use of public transport to work.

The two remaining clusters (Clusters 20 and 21) each consist of five English districts. They differ most strongly from the Scottish clusters in the average size of house and in a higher proportion of large houses; consequently overcrowding is less frequent. Of the two clusters *Cluster 20* has a very young population age structure, a higher social class structure and more owner-occupiers. Its five districts were centred on large New Towns which expanded rapidly in the 1970s – Basildon, Blyth Valley, Milton Keynes, Redditch and Tamworth. In *Cluster 21*, on the other hand, four of the five districts contain older New Towns (Corby, Halton, Harlow, Stevenage) and one district (The Wrekin) contains another of the more recently developed New Towns. This cluster is more industrial than Cluster 20.

Family 6A: Parts of Inner London
This family consists of three clusters and 4 per cent of the population; it contains 11 districts, ten of which are London boroughs; the exception is Slough.

This family is dissimilar to any of the other families – if not so much so as Family 6B. In tenure, in housing amenities, and in household composition it has something in common with Family 6B although generally is less extreme; in terms of social composition or of age structure it is definitely different. It has much the highest proportion of all the families of people born in the African New Commonwealth countries, and the proportion born in India or Pakistan is also high though exceeded by Family 4A *(traditional manufacturing areas)*.

Clusters of Family 6A (C25-C27)
Although there are only 11 areas in the family they are different enough to form three clusters. Of the three, Clusters 26 and 27 are the more similar; Cluster 25 is the odd one out as the dendogram shows. This is also apparent from their geographical composition for *Clusters 26* and *27* include eight Inner London boroughs (but not the central ones which are in Family 6B) whereas *Cluster 25* is more of a mixture, consisting of Ealing, Hounslow, and Slough. All three clusters have a large New Commonwealth-born population but in Clusters 26 and 27 the proportion of those born in Africa and the Caribbean are especially large.

Cluster 27 has fewer owner-occupiers and a lower social profile than Cluster 26; together with a relatively smaller New Commonwealth population. Whereas Cluster 25 differs from both Cluster 26 and 27 in having a fairly average social profile and housing tenure structure. Single non-pensioner households were less common, shared amenities were less common, the age structure was more even and so on.

Family 6B: Central London

This family consists of five well-known Central London boroughs (Camden, Hammersmith and Fulham, Kensington and Chelsea together with the Cities of London and Westminster) which form a single cluster (Cluster 28). The family is very different to any of the other families – even to Family 6A *(Inner London)*. Only 1 per cent of the population is included.

Many of the 35 variables used in deriving the population are either a maximum or minimum for this family (compared with other families). Thus there are very few children but many young adults; and the tenure pattern is for few owner-occupiers and much rented accommodation. Likewise the social structure is unusual and the service industries are more important than in any other family. The number of students, the number of single non-pensioner households, and of changes of addresses is high. In short, the combination of bed-sitters, *pied-à-terres* and the general economics of living in these districts have produced a combination of exceptional characteristics unlike those in the rest of London or any other part of the country.

81

Tables for Chapter 2

The 'family' and 'cluster' areas described above were used in Tables 3 to 5 below:—

Table 1
Rates of disorder by standard region per 100,000 population (excluding former Met. County areas and GLC)

	Incidents	rate per total population	rate per popn. 15-24 years
Yorks and Humber	18	1.20	7.78
South East	101	1.10	7.21
South West	40	0.94	2.75
East Anglia	16	0.87	5.92
East Midlands	33	0.87	5.65
West Midlands	18	0.73	4.81
North West	4	0.18	1.15
North	2	0.14	0.85
Wales	3	0.11	0.72

N.B. The total number of ACPO incidents is 251. Three could not be allocated to an area and thirteen seem to fall in Metropolitan areas.

Table 2
Rates of disorder by county (per 100,000 population)

	Incidents	rate per total population	rate per popn. 15-24 years
Oxfordshire	13	2.56	15.57
Berkshire	16	2.39	14.70
Surrey	17	2.15	14.25
Suffolk	12	2.03	14.00
North Yorkshire	13	2.00	13.20
Hampshire	26	1.80	11.03
Cornwall	6	1.43	10.51
Leicestershire	12	1.44	9.07
Devon	13	1.40	9.72

Table 3
Public disorder outside the metropolitan areas

Family areas	Incidents	Population	Rates per million
1A Established high status areas	23	7,605,840	3.0
1B Higher status growth areas	46	4,574,907	10.0
2A More rural areas	58	5,331,813	10.8
2B Resort and retirement areas	15	2,626,094	5.7
3 Mixed, town and country, with some areas of industry	72	11,996,909	6.0
4A Traditional manufacturing areas	8	5,232,240	1.5
4B Service centres and cities	24	7,005,183	3.4
5 Areas with much local authority housing	1	1,246,536	0.8
6A Parts of inner London	1	2,301,875	0.4
6B Central London	—	600,199	0.0
	248		

Table 4
Disorder incidents recorded in ACPO report by CACI 'cluster areas'

Clusters	Incidents	Population	Rates per million
Established high status areas			
1 (1A) Commuting areas	15	1,785,170	8.4
2 (1A) Suburban areas	8	3,809,024	2.1
3 (1A) Outer London	0	2,011,646	0.0
Higher status growth areas			
4 (1B) Smaller, less urbanised, growth areas	28	2,149,369	11.5
5 (1B) Larger, more urbanised, growth areas	18	2,149,369	8.3
More rural areas			
6 (2A) Rural areas with transient population	7	339,557	20.6
7 (2A) Rural Scotland	0	25,525	0.0
8 (2A) Remoter rural areas of England and Wales	29	2,578,426	11.2
9 (2A) Less remote mainly rural areas of England and Wales	22	2,388,305	9.2
Resort and Retirement areas			
10 (2B) Resort and retirement areas	15	2,626,094	5.7
Mixed, town and country areas with some industry			
11 (3) More rural areas with industry	34	3,387,830	10.0

Table 4
Disorder incidents recorded in ACPO report by CACI 'cluster areas'—continued

Clusters	Incidents	Population	Rates per million
Mixed, town and country areas with some industry			
12 (3) Towns with some surrounding country	28	3,765,468	7.4
13 (3) More industrial areas	10	4,635,278	2.1
14 (3) South Wales valleys	0	208,333	0.0
Traditional manufacturing areas			
15 (4A) The Black Country and similar	5	2,041,197	2.4
16 (4A) Pennine towns and similar	3	3,191,043	0.9
Service centres and cities			
17 (4B) Cities and more industrial service centres	3	4,542,345	0.6
18 (4B) Scottish service centres and Greenwich	0	209,873	0.0
19 (4B) Less industrial service centre	21	2,252,965	9.3
Areas with much local authority housing			
20 (5) More recent New Towns in England	1	482,879	2.0
21 (5) Maturer New Towns in England	0	450,670	0.0
22 (5) Scottish industrial areas	0	172,991	0.0
23 (5) Scottish mixed areas	0	0	0.0
24 (5) Glasgow and Tower Hamlets	0	139,996	0.0
Parts of Inner London			
25 (6A) Ealing, Hounslow and Slough	1	574,330	1.7
26 (6A) Brent, Haringey and Lambeth	0	698,031	0.0
27 (6A) Eastern boroughs	0	1,029,514	0.0
Central London			
28 (6B) Central London	0	600,199	0.0

* rates per million

** for full explanation of areas see Appendix A

*** This table gives all cluster areas in England, Wales and Scotland. Since incidents
collated were only in 'non-metropolitan' areas (see Map 1) some cluster areas have no
incidents recorded.

Appendix B: Area definitions used in this study.

1 The different pieces of research used in Chapter 3 use different area boundaries, mainly relating to how it was possible to retrieve the data. It may lead to some confusion however if, when talking about a type of research for a particular area, that area has not been sufficiently defined.

2 The following boundaries were used:

i Background Socio-Demographic (CACI) Data

Cowplain	1.5	KM Radius of Centre
Gravesend	1.7	KM Radius of Centre
Woking	4.5	KM Radius of Centre
Guildford	4.65	KM Radius of Centre
Sudbury	2.0	KM Radius of Centre
Haverhill	1.5	KM Radius of Centre

ii Violence Against the Person Statistics

These figures were produced by the (S1) Statistics Division. The figures for Woking and Guildford are based on Police Subdivisions, but the other four towns' figures relate specifically to the town boundaries, though Cowplain, as with the rest of the analysis, also includes Waterlooville.

iii Message-Pad Analysis

The *areas* roughly correspond to those defined in the observation study. In all cases they were somewhat smaller than the relevant police subdivisions – outlying communities being left out. **Cowplain** (in Cosham subdivision) included most incidents copied to Cowplain police station from Fratton control room, and besides Cowplain itself covered Waterlooville, Leigh Park and Horndean. **Gravesend** excluded Northfleet and Meopham. **Woking and Guildford** included most of their respective subdivisions save for outlying villages. **Haverhill and Sudbury** both comprised part of Sudbury subdivision; incidents selected were confined to the towns themselves.

iv Observational Data

The areas upon which field work was concentrated were:

Cowplain – Waterlooville, Horndean, North Cowplain, Wecock Farm Estate

Gravesham – Gravesend town centre

Woking – Mainly Woking town centre, with some visits to Horsell and West Byfleet

Guildford – Guildford town centre

Sudbury – Sudbury town centre

Haverhill – Haverhill town centre

3 Although these data are not coincident at all points, they cover roughly the same geographic area and it is felt that no sharpness of analysis has been lost.

Appendix C: Demographic and social data for study sites together with violence against the person tables

Table 1   1986 Age Profile for 15-19 and 20-24 cohorts

Location	Age	% Proportion of Pop.	86 Rate c/w County	86 Rate c/w Eng & Wales
*Cowplain	15-19	7.9	99	101
	20-24	7.5	87	91
Gravesend	15-19	8.3	108	106
	20-24	8.4	107	102
*Woking	15-19	7.5	99	96
	20-24	8.2	110	100
Guildford	15-19	7.3	96	94
	20-24	7.2	97	88
*Haverhill	15-19	9.4	131	120
	20-24	9.0	111	110
Sudbury	15-19	8.8	123	113
	20-24	8.4	104	102

Table 2   1986 Age Profile for 15-19 and 20-24 cohorts. Males only

Location	Age	% Proportion of Pop.	86 Rate c/w County	86 Rate c/w Eng & Wales
*Cowplain	15-19	8.5	123	101
	20-24	7.9	92	88
Gravesend	15-19	8.6	123	102
	20-24	8.7	107	97
*Woking	15-19	8.0	121	95
	20-24	8.3	102	92
Guildford	15-19	7.6	115	90
	20-24	7.4	91	82
*Haverhill	15-19	9.6	130	114
	20-24	9.3	109	103
Sudbury	15-19	9.1	123	108
	20-24	8.8	104	98

Table 2a
1981-1986 Age Comparison Profile for 15-19 and 20-24 Age Cohorts, Within the Six Towns, Males Only Compared to Whole Population

Location	Age	1981 % Prop of Pop	1986 % Prop of Pop	86 Rate c/w 81 Rate
*Cowplain	15-19	4.4	4.2	95
	20-24	2.8	3.9	140
Gravesend	15-19	4.5	4.2	94
	20-24	3.9	4.3	110
*Woking	15-19	4.2	4.0	95
	20-24	3.6	4.1	113
Guildford	15-19	4.0	3.6	90
	20-24	3.8	3.5	94
*Haverhill	15-19	4.3	4.8	110
	20-24	3.7	4.6	124
Sudbury	15-19	4.0	4.5	113
	20-24	3.1	4.3	138

Table 2b
Comparison of Towns with Change Rates for Respective Counties and England and Wales, Males only

Location	Age	% Change in Population 1981-1986	Diff'ce c/w County Change	Diff'ce c/w E & W Change
*Cowplain	15-19	− 1.1	+23.9	+ 6.5
	20-24	+44.6	+36.2	−39.1
Gravesend	15-19	− 8.2	−10.0	− 0.6
	20-24	+ 7.5	− 9.4	−14.9
*Woking	15-19	0.0	−17.0	− 7.6
	20-24	+19.6	+27.5	+14.1
Guildford	15-19	− 8.5	+ 8.5	− 0.9
	20-24	− 4.0	+ 3.9	− 9.5
*Haverhill	15-19	+18.1	+22.8	+25.7
	20-24	+32.3	+ 9.3	+26.8
Sudbury	15-19	+18.6	+23.3	+26.2
	20-24	+45.2	+22.2	+39.7

Table 2c Proportionate Change in Relevant Counties and England & Wales Males Only

Eng & Wales	15-19	− 7.6%
	20-24	+ 5.5%
Kent	15-19	−18.2%
	20-24	+16.9%
Hants	15-19	−25.0%
	20-24	+ 8.4%
Suffolk	15-19	− 4.7%
	20-24	+23.0%
Surrey	15-19	−17.0%
	20-24	− 7.9%

Table 3 Profile of Ethnic Origin

Location	% Ethnic Proportion	% Proportion by Ethnicity c/w County	Proportion by Ethnicity c/w Eng & Wales
*Cowplain			
Eire	0.5	68	42
W.I.	0.1	56	17
I.S.C.	0.3	54	23
O.N.C.	1.5	121	125
Else	1.9	78	79
Gravesend			
Eire	1.2	164	100
W.I.	0.2	163	33
I.S.C.	5.4	661	415
O.N.C	0.9	100	75
Else	1.6	76	67
*Woking			
Eire	1.2	100	100
W.I.	0.2	97	33
I.S.C.	1.8	229	138
O.N.C.	1.2	106	100
Else	5.7	131	238
Guildford			
Eire	1.1	90	92
W.I.	0.2	96	33
I.S.C.	0.6	79	46
O.N.C.	1.2	108	100
Else	4.1	93	171
*Haverhill			
Eire	1.1	211	92
W.I.	0.2	58	33
I.S.C.	0.4	109	31
O.N.C.	0.7	133	58
Else	1.9	38	79
Sudbury			
Eire	1.2	237	100
W.I.	0.1	36	17
I.S.C.	0.3	84	23
O.N.C.	0.5	98	42
Else	1.5	31	63

Table 3a Ethnic Proportions

E and W		Kent %	Hants %	Suffolk %	Surrey %
Eire	1.2	0.8	0.8	0.5	1.2
W.I.	0.6	0.1	0.2	0.3	0.2
I.S.C.	1.3	0.8	0.6	0.3	0.8
O.N.C.	1.2	0.9	1.2	0.5	1.2
Else	2.4	2.1	2.5	5.0	4.4

KEY

Eire	Republic of Ireland
W.I.	West Indian
I.S.C.	Indian Sub-continent
O.N.C.	Other New Commonwealth
Else	All Other Ethnic Categories

Table 4 1988 Unemployment Rates for Towns Compared with Relevant Counties

Location	% Proportion Unemployed	Rate c/w County	Rate c/w Eng & Wales
*Cowplain	5.5	101	63
Gravesend	9.9	164	114
*Woking	2.3	100	26
Guildford	2.6	112	30
*Haverhill	5.5	102	63
Sudbury	5.7	106	66

Table 4a 1986-1988 Change in Unemployment Rates for Towns Compared with Relevant Counties

Location	% Change in Proportion Unemployed	Rate c/w County	Rate c/w Eng & Wales
*Cowplain	−3.5	113	121
Gravesend	−5.1	131	176
*Woking	−1.8	90	62
Guildford	−2.4	120	83
*Haverhill	−4.3	154	148
Sudbury	−3.9	139	134

Table 5 Proportion of Council Houses for Towns Compared to Respective Counties and England & Wales

Location	% Proportion of Council Households	Rate c/w County	Rate c/w Eng & Wales
*Cowplain	22.2	88	72
Gravesend	36.4	156	118
*Woking	21.2	105	69
Guildford	28.5	142	93
*Haverhill	60.1	230	195
Sudbury	36.4	140	118

Table 6 Proportion of Poor Class Council Houses (Acorn Group G), Proportion of Mixed Inner City Homes (Group H), Proportion of Non-family Homes (Acorn Group I) and the number of Relatively Affluent Houses (Groups B and J) for Towns Compared to Respective Counties and England & Wales

Location	% Proportion of Households	Rate c/w County	Rate c/w Eng & Wales
*Cowplain			
B	44.9	199	295
G	8.2	344	158
H	0.0	0	0
I	0.0	0	0
J	26.9	123	161
Gravesend			
B	8.0	41	53
G	9.2	492	177
H	10.2	1806	261
I	5.4	199	104
J	13.3	76	80
*Woking			
B	18.8	113	124
G	0.7	262	13
H	3.9	1367	100
I	3.4	97	65
J	43.2	99	259
Guildford			
B	10.9	65	72
G	0.0	0	0
H	0.0	0	0
I	8.4	240	162
J	32.9	76	197
*Haverhill			
B	16.4	100	108
G	0.0	0	0
H	0.0	0	0
I	0.0	0	0
J	0.0	0	0
Sudbury			
B	19.4	118	128
G	1.8	229	35
H	0.0	0	0
I	1.8	140	35
J	5.3	39	32

Table 7
**Socio-economic Group Compositions for Towns Compared to Respective Counties and
England & Wales for Total Persons Aged 16+ in Employment**

Location	% Proportion of Population	Rate c/w County	Rate c/w Eng & Wales
*Cowplain			
1	19.6	113	117
2	38.2	116	118
3	17.6	81	72
4	14.7	90	78
5	2.9	55	51
6	7.0	109	350
Gravesend			
1	13.3	73	80
2	31.8	95	98
3	27.0	113	110
4	18.3	107	97
5	8.1	158	142
6	1.5	72	75
*Woking			
1	27.4	103	164
2	37.4	100	116
3	17.2	97	70
4	13.3	100	71
5	3.4	102	60
6	1.3	79	65
Guildford			
1	22.0	83	132
2	39.5	105	122
3	19.7	112	80
4	13.1	99	70
5	4.0	118	70
6	1.6	98	80
*Haverhill			
1	9.7	62	58
2	20.5	73	63
3	34.0	134	138
4	27.8	136	149
5	6.5	118	114
Sudbury 6	1.6	30	80
1	14.7	94	88
2	23.5	84	73
3	29.8	118	121
4	26.7	131	143
5	4.9	89	86
6	0.4	8	20

KEY

	Class 1	Professional and Managerial
	Class 2	Non-manual
	Class 3	Skilled Manual
	Class 4	Semi-skilled
	Class 5	Unskilled
	Class 6	Armed Forces/Unstated

Table 8
Crime Profile for Violence against the Person. Towns Compared to their Respective Counties 1983-1987

Location	% Rate of Increase	% County Rate of Increase	c/w County Rate
*Cowplain	+112	+21	533
Gravesend	+ 32	+34	94
*Woking	+ 76	+35	217
Guildford	+ 25	+35	71
*Haverhill	+ 26	+43	60
Sudbury	+200	+43	465

Table 9
Crime Profile for Violence against the Person for Towns in Relation to Male Population Compared to their Respective Counties 1983-1987

Location	% Change per 1000 for Town '83-'87	% Change per 1000 for County '83-'87	c/w County Rate
*Cowplain	+105	+19	553
Gravesend	+ 34	+32	106
*Woking	+ 65	+36	181
Guildford	+ 22	+36	61
*Haverhill	+ 17	+37	46
Sudbury	+183	+37	495

Table 9a
Crime Profile for Violence against the Person for Towns in Relation to Male Population Compared to their Respective Counties 1983-1987

Location	Rate per 1000 '83	Rate per 1000 '87	County Rate per 1000 '83	County Rate per 1000 '87
*Cowplain	6.3	12.8	3.9	4.7
Gravesend	9.2	12.4	3.2	4.2
*Woking	4.0	6.7	2.5	3.4
Guildford	6.0	7.3	2.5	3.4
*Haverhill	10.6	12.5	3.6	5.0
Sudbury	1.9	5.6	3.6	5.0

Appendix D:
Police message-pad data

Table 1
Absolute incident rates per weekend by area

area	drink/ licensed premises		violence		damage		noise		rowdiness		all incidents	
absolute weekend rate of incidents mentioning												
Haverhill	1.4	(13)	2.7	(24)	3.0	(27)	0.4	(4)	1.7	(15)	7.0	(63)
Sudbury	0.4	(4)	2.0	(18)	3.2	(29)	0.0	(0)	0.3	(3)	5.7	(51)
Woking	2.4	(22)	3.9	(35)	1.6	(14)	0.7	(6)	7.1	(64)	9.9	(89)
Guildford	3.6	(32)	4.2	(38)	1.0	(9)	0.8	(7)	3.4	(31)	10.0	(90)
Cowplain	1.8	(16)	3.1	(28)	0.8	(7)	1.0	(9)	2.1	(19)	6.3	(57)
Gravesend	3.0	(27)	5.0	(45)	2.4	(22)	1.7	(15)	3.8	(34)	10.8	(97)
average of above area rates	2.1	(114)	3.5	(188)	2.0	(108)	0.8	(41)	3.1	(166)	8.3	(447)

Source: message pads. Number of incidents = 447. Rates for individual areas are the average over 9 weekends; the rates for all areas are the average over 9 weekends and 6 areas. The figures in brackets are the raw numbers of incidents in the 9 weekend period. Each weekend lasted from 0601 Friday to 2400 Sunday.

Drink/licensed premises refers to incident reports on the message pad mentioning drink, drunkenness or licensed premises. Violence refers to assault, fighting, threat, offensive weapon, injury, clash with police; most incidents thus classed as violent involved assault or fighting. An incident report may have mentioned more than one feature (eg violence and damage), so the rates for the individual features sum to a figure greater than the rate for all incidents.

94

Table 2
Population-adjusted incident rates, by area, for weekends and peak hours

area		rate per thousand males aged 15-24 for incidents mentioning		
		drink/ licensed premises	violence	all incidents
Haverhill	W	.86	1.67	4.31
	P	.25	.19	.49
Sudbury	W	.25	1.22	3.49
	P	.12	.12	.25
Woking	W	.38	.61	1.56
	P	.06	.11	.17
Guildford	W	.70	.82	1.96
	P	.08	.12	.27
Cowplain	W	.91	1.56	3.18
	P	.20	.45	.50
Gravesend	W	.84	1.40	3.01
	P	.11	.17	.39
Average	W	.66	1.21	2.92
of above	P	.14	.19	.35
area rates				

Source: message pads/population data. The message pads yielded 447 incidents over 9 weekends. W is the rate per weekend, P the rate at the peak hour, averaged over the 9 weekends, which was usually 2301-2400 on a Friday or a Saturday. The populations were as follows:

Cowplain   (1.5   km radius) young males 15-24 1,982
Gravesend (1.7   km radius)   ,,   3,586
Woking   (4.5   km radius)   ,,   6,358
Guildford   (4.65 km radius)   ,,   5,116
Haverhill   (1.5   km radius)   ,,   1,625
Sudbury   (2.0   km radius)   ,,   1,634

The radii were derived from analysis done by CACI and the populations taken from CACI's 1986 population update.

Appendix E:
Results of drinking survey

Table 1
Drinking frequency of residents of Woking and Guildford compared with National Estimates

	Guildford	Woking	Nationally	(Nationally non-met)
	%	%	%	%
Almost every day	23	23	9	10
3 or 4 times a week	37	28	32	34
At least once a week	27	27	30	31
Once a fortnight	3	7	10	8
Once a month	6	5	6	6
Less often	1	2	8	8
Never (non-drinker)	3	7	5	3
Base (residents only)	663	670	393	248

Table 2
Amount drunk on Friday evening by residents of Woking and Guildford compared with National Estimates

	Guildford	Woking	Nationally	(Nationally non-met)
	%	%	%	%
Nothing	35	40	54	50
1-4 units	17	18	19	20
5-8 units	15	13	10	12
9-12 units	13	16	11	12
13-16 units	10	7	4	5
17+ units	10	7	3	2
Base (residents only)	663	670	393	248

Table 3
Average amount drunk on Friday evening compared with National Estimates

	Guildford	Woking	Nationally	(Nationally non-met)
*UNITS	6.7	5.6	3.4	3.5
Base (residents only)	663	670	393	248

*One unit of alcohol is roughly equivalent to half a pint of beer or one glass of wine.

Table 4
Amount drunk on Saturday evening by residents of Woking and Guildford compared with National Estimates

	Guildford	Woking	Nationally	(Nationally non-met)
	%	%	%	%
Nothing	31	38	45	43
1-4 units	21	16	24	26
5-8 units	14	13	10	10
9-12 units	15	17	9	10
13-16 units	10	7	5	6
17+ units	10	9	7	6
Base (residents only)	663	670	393	248

Table 5
Average amount drunk on Saturday evening compared with National Estimates

	Guildford	Woking	Nationally	(Nationally non-met)
UNITS	7.0	6.1	4.6	4.5
Base (residents only)	663	670	393	248

Table 6
Amount drunk on heaviest drinking night (Friday or Saturday) compared with National Estimates

	Guildford	Woking	Nationally	(Nationally non-met)
	%	%	%	%
Nothing	15	21	34	30
1-4 units	23	22	23	26
5-8 units	17	15	13	13
9-12 units	19	23	13	15
13-16 units	13	9	8	8
17+ units	14	11	9	8
Base (residents only)	663	670	393	248

Table 7
Average amount drunk by locals compared with outsiders (Saturday)

	Guildford		Woking	
	Locals	Outsiders	Locals	Outsiders
UNITS	10.5	9.5	8.8	8.1
Base (those who were out in Guildford/ Woking on Saturday night)	362	71	320	39

Table 8
Type of place visited on Friday night by heavy and light drinkers*

	Guildford		Woking	
	Light	Heavy	Light	Heavy
	%	%	%	%
Pub	68	85	66	79
Club	8	11	6	4
Disco	1	4	2	3
Wine bar	10	8	5	2
Hotel	4	2	2	1
Restaurant	3	3	1	2
Outside in street/sq/park	2	3	2	1
Own home	4	4	9	8
Someone else's home	6	11	8	10
Other	2	3	1	2
Base (those who were out in Guildford/ Woking on Friday night)	211	241	188	194

*Heavy drinkers are defined here as those who drank 9 or more units when they were
out on either Friday or Saturday night.

Table 9
**Average amount drunk on heaviest drinking night compared with national estimates
for different age groups**

	Guildford	Woking	Nationally
16-17 year olds	6.9	5.6	2.8
18-24 year olds	9.4	8.4	7.0
Base (residents only)	663	670	393

Table 10
Comparison of the proportions of different age groups drinking in pubs on either Friday or Saturday night

	Yes %	No %
16-17 year olds	32	68
18-24 year olds	52	48
Base	1048	753

Table 11
Number of fights or disturbances involving groups of people witnessed in past year

	Guildford %	Woking %
None	49	56
1-5	29	29
6-10	8	7
11-15	3	2
16+	11	6
Base	834	661

Table 12
Drinking involved in the incident

	Guildford %	Woking %
Yes	83	83
No	6	9
Not sure/DK	11	7
Base (incidents witnessed, 3 most recent included)	1103	742

Table 13
Number of people involved

	Guildford %	Woking %
1-5	42	44
6-10	26	21
11-20	11	16
21+	8	10
Not sure/DK	12	9
Base (incidents witnessed, 3 most recent included)	1103	742

Table 14
Anyone hurt during the most serious incident*

	Guildford %	Woking %
Yes	52	53
No	28	28
Don't know	20	18
Base (incident where most people involved)	436	298

*'Most serious' incident is defined as that involving most people out of the three most recent witnessed.

Table 15
Any property damaged during the incident

	Guildford %	Woking %
Yes	19	26
No	62	62
Don't know	19	13
Base (incident where most people involved)	436	298

Table 16
Locals or outsiders involved in incident

	Guildford %	Woking %
Mainly locals	35	55
Mainly outsiders	19	14
Both	17	14
Don't know	30	17
Base (incident where most people involved)	436	298

Table 17
Type of people involved in the incident

	Guildford %	Woking %
Soldiers/Squaddies	75	44
Youths/young people/teenagers	18	18
Hooligans/yobs	5	7
(Just) ordinary people	8	3
Don't know/Can't remember	4	1
Other answers	2	26
Base (where 'outsiders' involved in incident)	161	82

Percentages do not add to 100 as respondents could give more than one answer.

Table 18
Proportion of respondents involved in any incident

	Guildford %	Woking %
Involved	15	10
Not involved	85	90
Base	834	661

Table 19
Comparison of 'involved' and not involved by age, left full time education

	Involved %	Not involved %
16-17	72	49
18-21	8	19
22+	2	4
Still at school	18	28
Base	207	1279

Table 20
Comparison of 'involved' and not involved by age group

	Involved %	Not involved %
16-17	33	23
18-24	67	77
Base	207	1279

Table 21
Comparison of 'involved' and not involved by work status

	Involved %	Not involved %
Employed	63	64
unemployed	19	8
FT education	18	28
Base	207	1279

Table 22
Comparison of 'involved' and not involved by SEG

	Involved %	Not involved %
Senior managerial/administrative or professional	—	—
Intermediate managerial/adminstrative or professional	1	4
Junior managerial/administrative or professional, supervisory, clerical and also small traders	21	27
Skilled manual workers	27	27
Semi-skilled and unskilled manual workers	38	30
Casual workers, long-term unemployed (over 2 months) with no other earner in the household	—	—
Refused/insufficient information	13	12
Base (excludes those in ft education)	172	924

Table 23
Comparison of 'involved' and not involved by whether heavy or light drinker

	Involved %	Not involved %
Heavy	64	38
Light	36	62
Base	207	1279

102

Appendix F: Changes in numbers of licensed premises in petty sessional divisions relating to the six towns, 1982-3 compared to 1985-6.

	PUBLIC HOUSE etc.		LICENSED CLUBS		REGISTERED CLUBS	
	82-83	85-86	82-83	85-86	82-83	85-86
HAVANT	78	91	25	19	37	36
GRAVESHAM	125	126	3	3	47	46
WOKING	75	82	6	4	69	70
GUILDFORD	187	183	2	3	156	148
ST EDMUNDSBURY	113	110	3	5	45	47
BABERGH N/A	—	—	—	—	—	—

Publications

* Out of Print.

9. *Exploration in after-care. I—After-care units in London, Liverpool and Manchester. Martin Silberman (Royal London Prisoners' Aid Society) and Brenda Chapman. II—After-care hostels receiving a Home Office grant. Ian Sinclair and David Snow (HORU). III—St. Martin of Tours House, Ayreh Leissner (National Bureau for Co-operation in Child Care). 1971. xi + 140pp. (11 340109 4).

10. A survey of adoption in Great Britain. Eleanor Grey in collaboration with Roland M. Blunden. 1971. ix + 168pp. (11 340110 8).

11. *Thirteen-year-old approved school boys in 1962. Elizabeth Field, W. H. Hammond and J. Tizard, 1971. xi + 46pp. (11 340111 6).

12. Absconding from approved schools R. V. G. Clarke and D. N. Martin. 1971. vi + 146pp. (11 340112 4).

13. An experiment in personality assessment of young men remanded in custody. H. Sylvia Anthony. 1972. viii + 79pp. (11 340113 2).

14. *Girl offenders aged 17-20 years. I—Statistics relating to girl offenders aged 17-20 years from 1960 to 1970. II—Re-offending by girls released from borstals or detention centre training. III—The problems of girls released from borstal training during their period on after-care. Jean Davies and Nancy Goodman. 1972. v + 77pp. (11 340114 0).

15. *The Controlled trial in institutional research-paradigm or pitfall for penal evaluators? R. V. G. Clarke and D. B. Cornish. 1972. v + 33pp. (11 340115 9).

16. *A survey of fine enforcement. Paul Softley. 1973. v + 65pp. (11 340116 7).

17. *An index of social environment—designed for use in social work research. Martin Davies. 1973. vi + 63pp. (11 340117 5).

18. *Social enquiry reports and the probation service. Martin Davies and Andrea Knopf. 1973. v + 49pp. (11 340118 3).

19. *Depression, psychopathic personality and attempted suicide in a borstal sample. H. Sylvia Anthony. 1973. viii + 44pp. (11 340119 1).

20. *The use of bail and custody by London magistrates' courts before and after the Criminal Justice Act 1967. Frances Simon and Mollie Weatheritt. 1974. vi + 78pp. (11 340120 5).

21. Social work in the environment. A study of one aspect of probation practice. Martin Davies, with Margaret Rayfield, Alaster Calder and Tony Fowles. 1974. ix + 151pp. (11 340121 3).

22. Social work in prison. An experiment in the use of extended contact with offenders. Margaret Shaw. 1974. vii + 154pp. (11 340122 1).

23. Delinquency amongst opiate users. Joy Mott and Marilyn Taylor. 1974. vi + 31pp. (11 340663 0).

24. IMPACT. Intensive matched probation and after-care treatment. Vol. I—The Design of the probation experiment and an interim evaluation. M. S. Folkard, A. J. Fowles, B. C. McWilliams, W. McWilliams, D. D. Smith, D. E. Smith and G. R. Walmsley. 1974. v + 54pp. (11 340664 9).

25. The approved school experience. An acount of boys' experiences of training under differing regimes of approved schools, with an attempt to evaluate the effectiveness of that training. Anne B. Dunlop. 1974. vii + 124pp. (11 340665 7).

26. *Absconding from open prisons. Charlotte Banks, Patricia Mayhew and R. J. Sapsford. 1975. vii + 89pp. (11 340665 5).

27. Driving while disqualified. Sue Kriefman. 1975. vi + 136pp. (11 340667 3).

28. Some male offenders' problems. I—Homeless offenders in Liverpool. W. McWilliams. II—Casework with short-term prisoners. Julie Holborn. 1975. x + 147pp. (11 340668 1).

29. *Community service orders. K. Pease, P. Durkin, I. Earnshaw, D. Payne and J. Thorpe. 1975. viii + 80pp. (11 340669 X).

30. Field Wing Bail Hostel: the first nine months. Frances Simon and Sheena Wilson. 1975. viii + 55pp. (11 340670 3).

31. Homicide in England and Wales 1967-1971. Evelyn Gibson. 1975. iv + 59pp. (11 340753 X).

32. Residential treatment and its effects on delinquency. D. B. Cornish and R. V. G. Clarke. 1975. vi + 74pp. (11 340672 X).

33. Further studies of female offenders. Part A: Borstal girls eight years after release. Nancy Goodman, Elizabeth Maloney and Jean Davies. Part B: The sentencing of women at the London Higher Courts. Nancy Goodman, Paul Durkin and Janet Halton. Part C: Girls appearing before a juvenile court. Jean Davies. 1976. vi + 114pp. (11 340673 8).

34. *Crime as opportunity. P. Mayhew, R. V. G. Clarke, A. Sturman and J. M. Hough. 1976. vii + 36pp. (11 340674 6).

---

* Out of Print.

35. The effectiveness of sentencing: a review of the literature. S. R. Brody. 1976. v+89pp. (11 340675 4).

36. IMPACT. Intensive matched probation and after-care treatment. Vol II—The results of the experiment. M. S. Folkard, D. E. Smith and D. D. Smith. 1976. xi+400pp. (11 340676 2).

37. Police cautioning in England and Wales. J. A. Ditchfield. 1976. vi+31pp. (11 340677 2).

38. Parole in England and Wales. C. P. Nuttall, with E. E. Barnard, A. J. Fowles, A. Frost, W. H. Hammond, P. Mayhew, K. Pease, R. Tarling and M. J. Weatheritt. 1977. vi+90pp. (11 340678 9).

39. Community service assessed in 1976. K. Pease, S. Billingham and I. Earnshaw. 1977. vi+29pp. (11 340679 7).

40. Screen violence and film censorship: a review of research. Stephen Brody. 1977. vii+179pp. (11 340680 0).

41. Absconding from borstals. Gloria K. Laycock. 1977. v+82pp. (11 340681 9).

42. Gambling: a review of the literature and its implications for policy and research. D. B. Cornish. 1987. xii+284pp. (11 340682 7).

43. Compensation orders in magistrates' courts. Paul Softley. 1978. v+41pp. (11 340683 5).

44. Research in criminal justice. John Croft. 1978. iv+16pp. (11 340684 3).

45. Prison welfare: an account of an experiment at Liverpool. A. J. Fowles. 1978. v+34pp. (11 340685 1).

46. Fines in magistrates' courts. Paul Softley. 1978. v+42pp. (11 340686 X).

47. Tackling vandalism. R. V. G. Clarke (editor), F. J. Gladstone, A. Sturman and Sheena Wilson (contributors). 1978. vi+91pp. (11 340687 8).

48. Social inquiry reports: a survey. Jennifer Thorpe. 1979. vi+55pp. (11 340688 6).

49. Crime in public view. P. Mayhew, R. V. G. Clarke, J. N. Burrows, J. M. Hough and S. W. C. Winchester. 1979. v+36pp. (11 340689 4).

50. *Crime and the community. John Croft. 1979. v+16pp. (11 340690 8).

51. Life-sentence prisoners. David Smith (editor), Christopher Brown, Joan Worth, Roger Sapsford and Charlotte Banks (contributors). 1979. iv+51pp. (11 340691 6).

52. Hostels for offenders. Jane E. Andrews, with an appendix by Bill Sheppard. 1979. v+30pp. (11 340692 4).

53. Previous convictions, sentence and reconviction: a statistical study of a sample of 5,000 offenders convicted January 1971. G. J. O. Phillpotts and L. B. Lancucki. 1979. v+55pp. (11 340693 2).

54. Sexual offences, consent and sentencing. Roy Walmsley and Karen White. 1979. vi+77pp. (11 340694 0).

55. Crime prevention and the police. John Burrows, Paul Ekblom and Kevin Heal. 1979. v+37pp. (11 340695 9).

56. Sentencing practice in magistrates' courts. Roger Tarling, with the assistance of Mollie Weatheritt. 1979. vii+54pp. (11 340696).

57. Crime and comparative research. John Croft. 1979. iv+16pp. (11 340697 5).

58. Race, crime and arrests. Philip Stevens and Carole F. Willis. 1979. v+69pp. (11 340698 3).

59. Research and criminal policy. John Croft. 1980. iv+14pp. (11 340699 1).

60. Junior attendance centres. Anne B. Dunlop. 1980. v+49pp. (11 340700 9).

61. Police interrogation: an observational study in four police stations. Paul Softley, with the assistance of David Brown, Bob Forde, George Mair and David Moxon. 1980. vii+67pp. (11 340701 7).

62. Co-ordinating crime prevention efforts. F. J. Gladstone. 1980. v+74pp. (11 340702 5).

63. Crime prevention publicity: an assessment. D. Riley and P. Mayhew. 1980. v+47pp. (11 340703 3).

64. Taking offenders out of circulation. Stephen Brody and Roger Tarling. 1980. v+46pp. (11 340704 1).

65. *Alcoholism and social policy: are we on the right lines? Mary Tuck. 1980. v+30pp. (11 340705 X).

66. Persistent petty offenders. Suzan Fairhead. 1981. vi+78pp. (11 340706 8).

67. Crime control and the police. Pauline Morris and Kevin Heal. 1981. v+71pp. (11 340707 6).

68. Ethnic minorities in Britain: a study of trends in their positions since 1961. Simon Field, George Mair, Tom Rees and Philip Stevens. 1981. v+48pp. (11 340708 4).

69. Managing criminological research. John Croft. 1981. iv+17pp. (11 340709 2).

* Out of Print.

70. Ethnic minorities, crime and policing: a survey of the experiences of West Indians and whites. Mary Tuck and Peter Southgate. 1981. iv+54pp. (11 340765 3).

71. Contested trials in magistrates' courts. Julie Vennard. 1982. v+32pp. (11 340766 1).

72. Public disorder: a review of research and a study in one inner city area. Simon Field and Peter Southgate. 1982. v+77pp. (11 340767 X).

73. Clearing up crime. John Burrows and Roger Tarling. 1982. vii+31pp. (11 340768 8).

74. Residential burglary: the limits of prevention. Stuart Winchester and Hilary Jackson. 1982. v+47pp. (11 340769 6).

75. Concerning crime. John Croft. 1982. iv+16pp (11 340770 X).

76. The British Crime Survey: First Report, Mike Hough and Pat Mayhew. 1983. v+62pp. (11 340789 6).

77. Contacts between police and public: findings from the British Crime Survey. Peter Southgate and Paul Ekblom. 1984. v+42pp. (11 340771 8).

78. Fear of crime in England and Wales. Michael Maxfield. 1984. v+51pp (11 340772 6).

79. Crime and police effectiveness. Ronald V. Clarke and Mike Hough. 1984. iv+33pp. (11 340773 4).

80. The attitudes of ethnic minorities. Simon Field. 1984. v+50pp. (11 340077 2).

81. Victims of crime: the dimensions of risk. Michael Gottfredson. 1984. v+54pp. (11 340775 0).

82. The tape recording of police interviews with suspects: an interim report. Carole Willis. 1984. v+45pp. (11 340776 9).

83. Parental supervision and juvenile delinquency. David Riley and Margaret Shaw. 1985. v+90pp. (11 340799 8).

84. Adult prisons and prisoners in England and Wales 1970-82: a review of the findings of social research. Joy Mott. 1985. vi+73pp. (11 340801 3).

85. Taking account of crime: key findings from the 1984 British Crime Survey. Mike Hough and Pat Mayhew. 1985. vi+115pp. (11 340810 2).

86. Implementing crime prevention measures. Tim Hope. 1985. vi+82pp. (11 340812 9).

87. Resettling refugees: the lessons of research. Simon Field. 1985. vi+62pp. (11 340815 3).

88. Investigating burglary: the measurement of police performance. John Burrows. 1986. v+36pp. (11 340824 2).

89. Personal violence. Roy Walmsley. 1986. vi+87pp. (11 340827 7).

90. Police public encounters. Peter Southgate with the assistance of Paul Ekblom. 1986. vi+150pp. (11 340834 X).

91. Grievance procedures in prisons. John Ditchfield and Clair Austin. 1986, vi+78pp. (11 340839 0).

92. The effectiveness of the Forensic Science Service. Malcolm Ramsay. 1987. v+100pp. (11 340842 0).

93. The police complaints procedure: a survey of complainants' views. David Brown. 1987. v+98pp. (11 340853 6).

94. The validity of the reconviction prediction score, Denis Ward. 1987. vi+40pp. (11 340682 X).

95. Economic aspects of the illicit drug market and drug enforcement policies in the United Kingdom. Adam Wagstaff and Alan Maynard. 1988. vii+156pp. (11 340883 8).

96. Schools, disruptive behaviour and delinquency: a review of research. John Graham. 1988. v+70pp. (11 340887 0).

97. The tape-recording of policy interviews with suspects: a second interim report. Carole Willis, John Macleod and Peter Naish. 1988. vii+97pp. (11 340888 9).

98. Triable-either-way cases: Crown Court or magistrates' court? David Riley and Julie Vennard. 1988. v+52pp. (11 340890 0).

99. Directing patrol work: a study of uniformed policing. John Burrows and Helen Lewis. 1988. v+66pp. (11 340891 9).

100. Probation day centres, George Mair. 1988. v+44pp. (11 340894 3).

101. Amusement machines: dependency and delinquency. John Graham. 1988. v+48pp. (11 340895 1).

102. The use and enforcement of compensation orders in magistrates' courts. Tim Newburn. 1988. v+48pp. (11 340896 X).

103. Sentencing practice in the Crown Court. David Moxon. 1988. v+90pp. (11 340902 8).

104. Detention at the police station under the Police and Criminal Evidence Act 1984. David Brown. 1989. v+76pp. (0 11 340908 7).

* Out of Print.

105. Changes in rape offences and sentencing. Charles Lloyd and Roy Walmsley. 1989. vi+53pp.
      (0 11 340910 9).
106. Concerns about rape. Lorna J. F. Smith. 1989. v+48pp. (0 11 340911 7).

ALSO

Designing out crime. R. V. G. Clarke and P. Mayhew (editors). 1980. vii+186pp.
(22 340732 7).
(This book collects, with an introduction, studies that were originally published in HORS 34,
47, 49, 55, 62 and 63 and which are illustrative of the situational approach to crime prevention.)
Policing today. Kevin Heal, Roger Tarling and John Burrows (editors). 1985. v+181pp.
(11 340800 5).
(This book brings together twelve separate studies on police matters produced during the last few
years by the Unit. The collection records some relatively little known contributions to the debate
on policing.)
Managing criminal justice: a collection of papers. David Moxon (editor). 1985. vi+222pp.
(11 340811 0).
(This book brings together a number of studies bearing on the management of the criminal justice
system. It includes papers by social scientists and operational researchers working within the
Research and Planning Unit, and academic researchers who have studied particular aspects of
the criminal process.)
Situational crime prevention: from theory into practice. Kevin Heal and Gloria Laycock
(editors). 1986. vii+166pp. (11 340826 9).
(Following the publication of *Designing Out Crime*, further research has been completed on the
theoretical background to crime prevention. In drawing this work together this book sets down
some of the theoretical concerns and discusses the emerging practical issues. It includes
contributions by Unit staff as well as academics from this country and abroad.)
Communities and crime reduction. Tim Hope and Margaret Shaw (editors). 1988. vii+311pp.
(11 340892 7).
(The central theme of this book is the possibility of preventing crime by building upon the
resources of local communities and of active citizens. The specially commissioned chapters, by
distinguished international authors, review contemporary research and policy on community
crime prevention.)
New directions in police training. Peter Southgate (editor). 1988. xi+256pp. (11 340889 7).
Training is central to the development of the police role, and particular thought and effort now
go into making it more responsive to current needs—in order to produce police officers who are
both effective and sensitive in their dealings with the public. This book illustrates some of the
thinking and research behind these developments.)

The above HMSO publications can be purchased from Government Bookshops or through booksellers.

The following Home Office research publications are available on request from the Home Office
Research and Planning Unit, 50 Queen Anne's Gate, London, SW1H 9AT.

Research Unit Papers (RUP)
  1. Uniformed police work and management technology. J. M. Hough. 1980.
  2. Supplementary information on sexual offences and sentencing. Roy Walmsley and Karen White.
      1980.
  3. Board of Visitor adjudications. David Smith, Claire Austin and John Ditchfield. 1981.
  4. Day centres and probations. Suzan Fairhead, with the assistance of J. Wilkinson-Grey. 1981.

---

* Out of Print.

Research and Planning Unit Papers (RPUP)

5. Ethnic minorities and complaints against the police. Philip Stevens and Carole Willis. 1982.
6. *Crime and public housing. Mike Hough and Pat Mayhew (editors). 1982.
7. *Abstracts of race relations research. George Mair and Philip Stevens (editors). 1982.
8. Police probationer training in race relations. Peter Southgate. 1982.
9. *The police response to calls from the public. Paul Ekblom and Kevin Heal. 1982.
10. City centre crime: a situational approach to prevention. Malcolm Ramsay. 1982.
11. Burglary in schools: the prospects for prevention. Tim Hope. 1982.
12. *Fine enforcement. Paul Softley and David Moxon. 1982.
13. Vietnamese refugees. Peter Jones. 1982.
14. Community resources for victims of crime. Karen Williams. 1983.
15. The use, effectiveness and impact of police stop and search powers. Carole Willis. 1983.
16. Acquittal rates. Sid Butler. 1983.
17. Criminal justice comparisons: the case of Scotland and England and Wales. Lorna J. F. Smith. 1983.
18. Time taken to deal with juveniles under criminal proceedings. Catherine Frankenburg and Roger Tarling. 1983.
19. Civilian review of complaints against the police: a survey of the United States literature. David C. Brown. 1983.
20. Police action on motoring offences. David Riley. 1983.
21. *Diverting drunks from the criminal justice system. Sue Kingsley and George Mair. 1983.
22. The staff resource implications of an independent prosecution system. Peter R. Jones. 1983.
23. Reducing the prison population: an explanatory study in Hampshire. David Smith, Bill Sheppard, George Mair and Karen Williams. 1984.
24. Criminal justice system model: magistrates' courts sub-model. Susan Rice. 1984.
25. Measures of police effectiveness and efficiency. Ian Sinclair and Clive Miller. 1984.
26. Punishment practice by prison Boards of Visitors. Susan Iles, Adrienne Connors, Chris May and Joy Mott. 1984.
27. *Reparation, conciliation and mediation. Tony Marshall. 1984.
28. Magistrates' domestic courts: new perspectives. Tony Marshall (editor). 1984.
29. Racism awareness training for the police. Peter Southgate. 1984.
30. Community constables: a study of policing initiative. David Brown and Susan Iles. 1985.
31. Recruiting volunteers. Hilary Jackson. 1985.
32. Juvenile sentencing: is there a tariff? David Moxon, Peter Jones and Roger Tarling. 1985.
33. Bring people together: mediation and reparation projects in Great Britain. Tony Marshall and Martin Walpole. 1985.
34. Remands in the absence of the accused. Chris May. 1985.
35. Modelling the criminal justice system. Patricia M. Morgan. 1986.
36. The criminal justice system model: the flow model. Hugh Pullinger. 1986.
37. Burglary: police actions and victims' views. John Burrows. 1986.
38. Unlocking community resources: four experimental government small grant schemes. Hilary Jackson. 1986.
39. The cost of discriminating: a review of the literature. Shirley Dex. 1986.
40. Waiting for Crown Court trial: the remand population. Rachel Pearce. 1987.
41. Children's evidence: the need for corroboration. Carol Hedderman. 1987.
42. A preliminary study of victim offender mediation and reparation schemes in England and Wales. Gwynn Davis, Jacky Boucherat and David Watson. 1987.
43. Explaining fear of crime: evidence from the 1984 British Crime Survey. Michael Maxfield. 1988.
44. Judgements of crime seriousness: evidence from the 1984 British Crime Survey. Ken Pease. 1988.
45. Waiting time on the day in magistrates' courts: a review of case listing practices. David Moxon and Roger Tarling (editors). 1988.
46. Bail and probation work: the ILPS temporary bail action project. George Mair. 1988.

* Out of Print.

47.   Police work and manpower allocation. Roger Tarling. 1988.
48.   Computers in the courtroom. Carol Hedderman. 1988.
49.   Data interchange between magistrates' courts and other agencies. Carol Hedderman. 1988.
50.   Bail and probation work II: the use of London probation/bail hostels for bailees. Helen Lewis
      and George Mair 1989.

* Out of Print.

Research Bulletin

The Research Bulletin is published twice a year and consists mainly of short articles relating to projects which are part of the Home Office Research and Planning Unit's research programme.

Printed in the United Kingdom for Her Majesty's Stationery Office.
Dd 291229, 4/89, C15, 3385/2, 16268